The New Birth

A Naturalistic View of Religious Conversion

The New Birth

A Naturalistic View of
Religious Conversion

by
Joe Edward Barnhart
and
Mary Ann Barnhart

Mercer University Press

Macon, Ga.

Some of the Scripture quotations in this publication are from the Revised Standard Version of the Bible, copyrighted 1946, 1952, © 1971, 1973 by the Division of Christian Education of the National Council of Churches of Christ in the U.S.A., and used by permission.

Library of Congress Cataloging in Publication Data

Barnhart, Joe E., 1931-
 The new birth.

 Bibliography: p. 165.
 Includes index.
 1. Conversion. I. Barnhart, Mary Ann, 1930-
II. Title.
BV4916.B324   248.2'4   81-9557
ISBN 0-86554-009-8   AACR2

9-27-88

For Janie and Romeo Greene

Foreword

It would be impossible to limit to a few the number of individuals who have enriched our understanding of the new birth process. Over the years, the Society for the Scientific Study of Religion, the American Academy of Religion, and various philosophical societies have provided us with opportunities to test some of the interpretations that eventually were woven into this book. Ideas from in-depth interviews with religious converts, from journal articles and professional papers, from scholarly books and our own systematic observations—all have fed into this study of religious conversion.

We wish to express our appreciation for those who have talked to us and corresponded with us about our work. By combing carefully through the manuscript, Edd Rowell of Mercer University Press prevented us from making several errors. In addition, Amelia Barclay and Bill Stembridge carefully read and corrected the galleys; and Pauline Coll and Edd Rowell read the final pages. But the touch of human fallibility remains despite the best of combined efforts. We believe our insights and interpretations will nevertheless prove rewarding and fruitful to the serious reader.

Table of Contents

Foreword ix

Introduction 1

   Bias and Objectivity 1
   Born Again—An Ancient Concept 2
   The Need for Meaning 3
   Can Only Believers Understand? 3
   Is Every Believer an Unbeliever? 4
   Understanding and Healthy Criticism 5
   Ourselves Twenty-Five Years Ago 6
   Three Positions 6

I. The Variety and Persistency of Religious Conversion 9

   An Incurably Religious Species 9
   The Problem of "Counterfeit" Conversion 11
   The Variety of Religious Conversions 12
   From Billy Graham to the Reverend Moon 13
   A Critical Question 13
   Undergoing Conversion at Several Levels 14
   How Many Changes Make A Conversion? 18
   Advancing a Theory 19
   Three Dimensions of Religious Conversion 19

II. The Psychological Dimension of the Second Birth 21

   The Importance and Limits of
     the Psychological Approach 21
   The Sense of Finitude 22
   The Moral Mode of Finitude 24
   The Emotional Mode of Finitude 27
   The Intellectual Mode of Finitude 28
   The Craving for Infallibility 29
   The Paradox of Psychology of Religion 32
   The Case of John Henry Newman 32
   The Question of Authority 33
   The Psychological States of John Henry Newman
     and John Wesley 35

The Storm Over Papal Infallibility 36
The Background of Theories and Presuppositions 37
The New Birth of Ernest Renan.........................38
The Old Faith and the New............................39
Comparing Renan and Newman 40
Renan's *Life of Jesus*................................41
The Conversion of Contemporary
    Roman Catholicism...............................41
The Conversion of Paul: A Paradigm Case 42
The Divided Self 43
Conflicting Directions of the Self 45
The Tragedy of Divided Loyalties 46
The Psychology of the Desperate Creature 47
Summary 48

III. *The Role of Vision and Voices in the New Birth* 49
Two Styles of Conversion..............................49
The Traumatic Conversion.............................50
The Appearance of the Deceased Husband 50
The Vision of the Apostle Peter 52
The Appearance of Christ 53
Reflection on Visions 55
Functional Dreams 56
Hearing and Obeying the Voices.......................57
The Bicameral Mind 57
The Decline of the Voices 59
The Return of the Golden Age 60
The Confusion of Voices 61
Controlling the Voices 62
Prophecy and the Rationalization Process 63
Paul's Three Control Mechanisms......................65
The Apostle Paul and the Reverend Moon 68
The Community and the Sacred Book...................70

IV. *The Social Womb* 71
Society and Religion: An Interaction 71
Collective Representations 71
The Social and Shifty Species..........................73
The Role of Religion to Generate Courage 74
Religion and the Grandiose 75
Terror in Religion....................................76

The Second Birth 77
The Discovery of Society 79
The New Birth as a Universal Phenomenon 80
Freely You Have Received 80
Pluralism 81
Summary 82

V. *The New Birth in Cultural Perspective* 83

Basic Religious Questions in a Pluralistic Society 83
Within the Sphere of Thought 84
Historical Relativism 85
Cultural Relativism 86
The Voice of the Authority Figure 88
The Messages of the Voices..............................90
Diverse Rites of Passage 90
The Message of the God 92
Social Sources of Theology 93
Moral Transcendence 95
Born Again—Mystical or Practical? 97
"Do I Really Believe?" 99

VI. *The Theological and Philosophical Dimensions
    of the New Birth* 103

The Crucial Question 103
A Problem of Theology 104
Levels of Genuineness 105
Revolution in Science and Religion......................107
The Development of Contradictions
    in the Hebrew Tradition 108
Applying the Belief-System 109
Extending the Belief-System 109
The Jewish Culture Confronting
    the Hellenistic Culture 110
The Pressure on Pharisaic Judaism 111
The New Cosmic Expectations 112
The New Birth of the Entire Universe 114
The Christian Son of God 116
Christ Supersedes the Law in
    the Theological Revolution 117
The Joy of a Released Prisoner 117
In the Tradition of Paul the Apostle 118
Metaphysical Disorientation.............................119

VII. *The Creation of New Desires* 121

What Dictates Our Desires? 121
The Case of Elizabeth Van Dyke........................ 122
Caused to Desire 122
How to Turn Freedom Into Slavery 124
Substituting of Desires 124
Reconstructing the Memories of the Old Life 125
Romantic Passion and Religious Conversion 126
Irresistible Grace 128
Flings 128
Nothing is the Same................................... 129
Everything Looks Different 131
A Fool for Christ...................................... 134
Guilt and the Loss of Commitment...................... 136
Hope and Commitment 138
The Flirt and the Proselytizing Agent 141
From Faith to Faith 142

VIII. *Brainwashing and Other Recruitment Methods* 145

The Oakland Family 145
A Question of Degree.................................. 149
Religious Indoctrination and Religious Education 149
Loss in Either Indoctrination or Education 149
Ambivalence About Education 150
Openness of Inquiry 150
The Question of Brainwashing 151
Brainwashing vs. Rational Method 152
Brainwashing, Conversion, and Radical Shift............. 153
Unfair Tactics and Methods 155
Conditioning, Conversion, and Brainwashing............. 156
Free Choice as Always Conditional 157
Independence of Mind 158
Freedom by Controls.................................. 159
Free Choice and Human Dignity 161
Beliefs and Tactics.................................... 161
Rational Inquiry and Emotional Desperation............. 163

Bibliography... 165

Index... 173

Introduction

Bias and Objectivity

Like gears in neutral, a mind without biases cannot travel far. Any serious study of religious conversion or the celebrated "born again" phenomenon will begin with preconceived notions. A number of public school principals and superintendents have been known to demand that teachers purge themselves of all biases and preconceptions before stepping into the classroom. This misconceived demand is itself based on a bias that deserves to be criticized in a separate book.

Having said that the study of religion invariably contains biases, we wish just as forcefully to say that religion can be studied objectively. Some school officials have insisted that history, biology, and other courses be studied objectively. Religion, they have gone on to add, cannot be studied objectively and therefore should not be permitted in the public schools.

In contrast to this bias, we contend that religion, history, biology, or any other area of study can be studied objectively. But if it is to be done, it must necessarily begin with biases. The objective study of religion, or of any other subject, does not require anyone to empty his mind or turn it into the proverbial blank (tabula rasa). It does, however, require openness of mind. What does this entail?

First, it requires us to give a hearing to biases that are not our own. Second, it requires us to expose systematically our own biases (as well as the other biases) to rigorous criticism and scrutiny. Every relevant view should be placed on the witness stand insofar as possible so that it may be both cross-examined and allowed to give its own "witness."

Total or complete objectivity is clearly impossible, since no one has the personal resources for considering all criticism and entertaining all rival or alternative views. Individuals may, nevertheless, significantly raise their present level of objectivity. The reader of this book will note that, like himself, we as the authors bring our biases with us. In the process of researching and writing, we have revised some of our original biases, surrendered others, retained some, and adopted new ones. We will offer some of the fruit of our relatively objective study of the phenomenon of religious conversion, a study that has demanded several years of our lives.

Born Again—An Ancient Concept

The idea of being "born again" is quite ancient—more ancient than Christianity or even Judaism. In time, we hope to show why "the new birth" has been so profoundly significant to the various societies of the world. Despite the serious and deep disagreements among them, all religions have some concept of the "new birth" or "rebirth." Why is this the case? And why has the concept been so central to all religions? One of the world's leading authorities on world religions suggests this: "If we look closely, we see that every human life is made up of a series of ordeals, of 'deaths', and of 'resurrections'."[1] In other words, the human preoccupation with the new birth arises out of the awareness that human life is very transitional and temporal. The sixth century B.C. philosopher Heraclitus noted that all things are in flux and nothing stays fixed. He likened everything alive to a flowing river and said that "you cannot step twice into the same river."[2]

Men and women have changed careers and jobs, joined new causes, become involved in romantic affairs, and undergone religious conversions of the most radical sort in the attempt to escape the relentless hounds of Time. They did not want the river of life to leave them behind, sitting in atrophy on the bank.

Our own naturalistic view of religious conversion must do more than assert that the supernaturalistic accounts are misleading and inherently obscure. It must, in addition, indicate positively and at least broadly how

---

[1]Mircea Eliade, *Rites and Symbols of Initiations: The Mysteries of Birth and Rebirth,* trans. W. R. Trask (New York: Harper and Row Torchbooks, 1958), p. 128.

[2]See Plato, *Cratylus* 402a.

it is that conversions come about in every generation and on every part of the globe. What are the principal ingredients of the "new birth"? What does religious conversion do for individuals, or at least promise to do? How does the "new birth" process function in society and how does it come about? These are questions that we have determined to deal with.

The Need for Meaning

Contending that economic forces alone cannot account for the survival of religion over the centuries, the noted student of religion Max Weber speaks of "an inner compulsion to understand the world as a meaningful cosmos and to take a position toward it."[3] In this book, we will show that one of the major functions of the new birth phenomenon in religion has been to provide believers with a kind of "map" of the cosmos and a key for locating themselves on this map. To be thus located is to find meaning and a place in life. To be sure, different religions draw maps that differ radically from one another. Even those people who claim to have no religion at all have nevertheless in the back of their minds a "map" or "picture" of the cosmos of which they are a part. This is necessary in order to enjoy a sense of orientation, which is the fundamental psychological difference between cosmos and chaos. People have sometimes been quite fierce about their religion because they believed that to lose it would be to lose their sense of direction, orientation, and meaning. For them, religion is the wall holding back the sea of chaos.

Can Only Believers Understand?

One of the claims that religious believers often make is that no one can understand their religion unless he first *believes in* its fundamental claims. These believers see themselves as explorers who have entered into a realm of reality that the outsider can never hope to understand or appreciate until he personally journeys there himself. Believers sometimes respond to their critics by asking, "Do you believe as we?" If the answer is "No," then the believers are likely to reply, "Well, you cannot understand unless you believe."

If it were actually true that only believers understand their religion, it would follow that people of different religious faiths could never *communicate* with one another about religion, since communication requires some understanding. Furthermore, if only believers in a particular religion can understand it, then it follows that evangelical

---

[3]Max Weber, *The Sociology of Religion,* trans. Talcott Parsons (Boston: Beacon Press, 1922), p. 117.

Christians could not *disagree* with Buddhists on religious matters because they would be unable to understand the Buddhist religion in the first place.

Is it true that a Baptist *cannot* understand the Buddhist religion or the Islamic faith? There are numerous Baptists, Presbyterians, Catholics, and other Christians who do not understand Buddhism or other world religions. But is this lack of understanding to be explained by the fact that these Christians do not *believe in* these other religions? It would seem that when believers sometimes say that no one but them can understand their own religion, they have implied conclusions which they themselves would not wish to draw.

The truth seems to be that neither outsiders nor insiders have the complete understanding of even one religion. Furthermore, it is possible for each to enrich and increase the understanding of the other. Unbelievers can learn from believers. And believers can sometimes learn from unbelievers things about their own religion, things that they might never have grasped otherwise.

Our point here is that the "outsider" cannot claim that only he enjoys an objective perspective from which to understand another person's religion. By the same token, neither does the "insider" enjoy the exclusive perspective from which to interpret his own conversion. What is required is better communication between the insider and the outsider in order to improve the understanding of each.

Is Every Believer an Unbeliever?

Every believer in the world is also an unbeliever. It is logically impossible for anyone to be a believer in all the religions or faiths of the world. A Baptist cannot consistently be a Muslim, Hindu or Catholic. Believers may perhaps share some common convictions, but there are other critical convictions which they cannot share if each is to hold sincerely to his own faith. Just because an evangelical Presbyterian believes as he does, he will *not* believe in a number of the major teachings of the denomination called the Church of Christ. To believe is also to *disbelieve*. Every insider is also an outsider.

In his article, "Oriental Balancing Act," a Christian pastor in Singapore lists various "superstitions" to which some of his Chinese neighbors adhere. The mere use of the word "superstitions" reveals that the pastor is an *unbeliever*. Believing as he does, he cannot consistently believe as they do on some very crucial matters. For example, he claims that many Chinese in Singapore believe that an individual can escape from evil spirits by running across a busy street in front of a car.

"Although the fleet-footed pedestrian may cause a few cars to squeal their brakes, the poor spirit is doubtless run over."[4] This Christian pastor either does not believe that there are evil spirits, or that if such spirits do exist they cannot be liquidated by automobile bumpers.

Believers sometimes complain that outsiders or unbelievers offer nothing but criticisms of their religion. This complaint fails to see that often the most severe criticisms of a religion come from believers themselves. Indeed, in some cases, insiders are in a favored position for offering criticisms of a certain kind. We refer here to criticism in its limited, but necessary, sense as the detection of apparent inconsistencies and contradictions. Criticism in this sense is a major factor leading to religious conversion.

Understanding and Healthy Criticism

Understanding is more than criticism; but without healthy criticism, understanding would degenerate to little more than repeating the same claim in other words. Genuine advances in understanding mean new insights, more comprehensive and more carefully formulated explanations, and improvement over previous explanations. But none of these advances would be possible if we should lose our sensitivity to inconsistencies and contradictions. Criticism is not an end in itself, for that would be only another form of dogmatism. Rather in its constructive and creative role, criticism must be rigorous and persistent if we are to fulfill our prior commitment to seek better understanding. It is this commitment to enrich the understanding and appreciation of the new birth phenomenon that motivates any critical analysis offered in this book.

Some of the most telling and effective criticisms of religion have been made by religious believers themselves. Or, quite often, when a religion finds itself under criticism, it discovers that the criticisms are coming from *another religion*. Every major religion has advanced criticisms of other religions. To be sure, some Hindus claim that they are exceptions to this, since they accept and absorb all other religions into Hinduism. But this claim is nothing less than a very subtle but severe criticism of Christianity, Islam, Buddhism, religious humanism, and all the other major religions. To claim to absorb all other religions is in effect to trim them down to fit into one's own scheme. Once they are cut down to fit this scheme, the other religions are no longer what they were.

---

[1]R. E. Finney, Jr., "Oriental Balancing Act," *Liberty: A Magazine of Religious Liberty,* 72:3 (May-June, 1977), 21.

Very often, criticisms of a particular religion will seem to originate from *within* the religion itself. Prophets, theologians, worshipers, laymen, or ministers sometimes feel strongly that there is something lacking in their own religion or at least that there is some inconsistency in it.

Criticism is necessarily evil for the insecure and for those who have something to conceal. But those who wish to enrich their understanding will welcome it even though at the time it might be upsetting and difficult to deal with. In Chapter 6 we will show how the Apostle Paul's religious outlook was changed drastically because of certain inconsistencies that he detected in his old outlook, criticisms which he could not ignore and which he felt needed to be dealt with radically. Religious conversion will be understood only on the surface if we ignore the role played in it by the individual's struggles with inconsistencies perceived within his own belief-system. Without a belief-system, human beings cannot function *at all.* But they become candidates for conversion if their belief-system is perceived by them as harboring servere contradictions. The human organism begins to scan the horizon searching unconsciously for a new boat to step into in case the old one begins to sink under the weight of its inconsistencies. In order to overcome this natural human tendency to scan, some religions, in their attempts to maintain their control, have been forced to attack the tendency to scan by labeling it as an act of betrayal and treason.

Ourselves Twenty-Five Years Ago

Looking back over our own religious venture, we asked ourselves this question, "If we had found this book on the new birth in our hands twenty-five or thirty years ago, what would our reaction to it have been after reading it?" We think that we could have followed the book well, or at least most of it. But we also think that it would have upset us. In addition, it would have challenged us to come to terms with some of its questions as well as its alternative views, many of which would have been quite new to us.

Beyond that, we are not sure at all as to how we would have responded to this book. But if it will challenge and stimulate the thinking of our readers today, we will judge that our goal in writing it has been attained.

Three Positions

We begin our inquiry by suggesting that there are roughly three positions as to what the "born again" phenomenon actually is and means. The first position states that the "new birth" is nothing other than an unfortunate *delusion* that a large number of people inflict on themselves. Some of those who take this position think that the delusion is mostly harmless, whereas others regard it as often quite disruptive of human development.

The second position, standing in strong opposition to the first, claims that being born again is not a delusion but a genuine *supernatural work* of God. Those who take this position insist further that there are certain requirements which must be met before this supernatural transformation can take place. However, among those who hold to this belief is a diversity of opinion as to exactly what these requirements are.

The third position states that it is a mistake to conclude that the new birth is nothing but a delusion. At the same time, according to this third position, the new birth is not a supernatural event or process, but a very complex personal process with at least three layers or dimensions—the psychological, the social, and the cultural. Included in the cultural dimension are theological and metaphysical doctrines which may or may not be warranted in what they assert but which nevertheless have a profound impact on the individual and society.

Chapter I

The Variety and Persistency
of Religious Conversion

An Incurably Religious Species

At a large university in the Southwest a professor of economics became increasingly curious about religious conversion when the son of his dearest friends suddenly converted to the Moonies. Without warning and to their shock, the parents received word that their son was in California, two thousand miles away from home, "serving the Lord" in a Moonie Commune. We met to talk with the parents for a number of hours after they had hired Ted Patrick to "deprogram" their son. Today, they cannot conceal their joy that their son has no desire to return to the Moonies.

But recently their hearts sank when they received news that Cynthia, the daughter of one of their nearby friends, had just returned to the Reverend Moon's Unification Church even though she had left the Moonies three years earlier. There is, of course, a certain tragedy in all of this. When twenty-seven-year-old Cynthia returned to the Moonies after having worked tirelessly for three years against them, her stunned friends and family asked "Why?" For some of them, the question was, "Why convert to the *Moonies?*" To others, the question was, "Why convert to *any* religion at all?" In May 1978 one of us flew to the Unification Theological Seminary in New York to talk there with the Moonie students and some of the faculty and to hear the very moving stories of young men and women whose parents had tried desperately to "deprogram" them. Before the New York trip, we had entertained Moonies in our home and met with them elsewhere in order to learn what we could about their religious conversion. In the summer of 1980 both of us flew to Hawaii to meet with both a number of students of new religious groups and a number of the seminary students and graduates of the Unification Theological Seminary. We were particularly interested in raising questions about the belief-system of this group, the life-style it fosters, and the conversion process experienced by its various members.

This is not a book on Sun Myung Moon's Unification Church or any other single religious group.* We will focus on the question of why people convert to a religion of any kind. Or, to be more explicit, our goal is to explore some of the highly significant conditions, consequences, and processes of religious conversion in general, as it cuts across a large variety of religious groups. The question, therefore, is not so much whether people *should* convert, but why and how they *do in fact* convert.

We will draw from our own study in theology and social theory, and combine that study with our many interviews with Mormons and Moonies, Catholics and charismatics, Jehovah's Witnesses and "born again" Southern Baptists, as well as other Christian and non-Christian believers. It will be fruitful to deal with the ordinary conversion as well as the bizarre, the smooth-flowing new birth as well as the traumatic.

The bizarre conversions take on a certain recognizable quality and structure of their own. We recall the aggressive atheist who seemed driven to convert virtually everyone to atheism until he himself converted to a strange mixture of Los Angeles Hinduism, magical beliefs, and ghost chasing. Saturated with his new-found faith, he lost none of his previous aggressiveness and zeal to convert everyone possible. In knowing him personally and studying him closely for a few years, we came to see that in certain striking ways the man was like both the aggressive fundamentalist preachers we had known in east Tennessee and the evangelistic Marxists we had talked with in Boston in the 1950's.

To say that a religious conversion is bizarre is not to say that we can make no sense of it as a psychological and social reality. Every manifestation of religion might appear quite bizarre to those who are unfamiliar with its internal structure. The point is to seek to understand

---

*Sociologists Anson Shupe, Jr., and David Bromley have shared with us many of their papers on the new religious movement. Their book *"Moonies" in America* (Beverly Hills: Sage Publications, 1979) is in our opinion currently the best sociological study of the Moonies. Their new book, *The New Vigilantes* (Sage, 1981), deals with the "anticult" phenomenon. Dr. Shupe has allowed us to have many days of his time to learn from his special research and insights.

the bizarre and to make sense of it by uncovering its context.

At the very outset we wish to state one of the conclusions of our search and study. It is this: For good or ill, the human species is incurably religious! Some people look upon religion as a disease. If it is in some sense a disease, then their only hope is to become "infected" with a strain that they can best live with emotionally, intellectually, and morally. Religion and religious conversions will endure in various forms or strains so long as the human species survives on this planet, or on any other planet for that matter. In the chapters of this book, we think it will become clear why there is no cure for religion. There are only various forms of it in which one can become involved.

Karl Marx professed to look for the day when the human race would overcome religion of every form. In fact, however, he helped to initiate one of the most sweeping religious movements of modern times. The writers in *The God that Failed*[1] provide vivid accounts of how they were converted to the religion of Marxism and how they were subsequently converted away from it. What we hope to do is to throw light on that powerful and precarious transition, that special period of in-betweenness, called religious conversion.

The Problem of "Counterfeit" Conversion

It is a fact that the very people who insist on the need for conversion are often quick to conclude that the conversions that many people have experienced are not genuine. New religious groups in particular are prone to regard the old-style conversion to be counterfeit at worst, inferior at best. In his book *Youth, Brainwashing and the Extremist Cults,* sociologist Ronald Enroth notes that some of the converts of new religious groups do not regard as authentic the conversion experiences of anyone outside their group. Pressed to account for the apparent religious conversion of the individual outside their group, they are likely to explain that the individual is under the power and direction of Satan. Professor Enroth is an evangelical Christian who, with a twist of irony, concludes that the new religious movements are themselves the work of Satan.[2]

In our book, we do not fall back on the Satan-hypothesis, but regard such an hypothesis as a hasty way to dismiss behavior that needs to be understood with greater insight. We were pleased to learn from some of his colleagues in sociology that Professor Enroth, after writing his book, had second thoughts about the scope of his own Satan-hypothesis. At the

---

[1]See Richard Crossman, ed., *The God that Failed* (New York: Bantam Books, 1952).

[2](Grand Rapids: Zondervan, 1977), pp. 13, 89, 119.

same time, the students at the Unification Theological Seminary have themselves grown reluctant to use the Satan-hypothesis to account for all their troubles and rivals.

The Variety of Religious Conversions

On 29 December 1977 in the San Francisco Bay area we talked at length with a young public relations employee of the Moonies. She told us of her conversion from her evangelical Missouri Lutheran Synod Church to active participation in the Unification Church. As we listened to her witness to the phenomenal success of the Unification Church, one of us asked her how she accounted for the phenomenal success of, for example, the Mormons. Later in this chapter we will indicate how she attempted to handle this question.

On 30 December 1977 while talking with a young man representing the Krishna Consciousness movement, one of us asked him to give his opinion of the Unification Church. Conspicuously uncomfortable in handling this request, the young man was at a loss to explain the Church's appeal and its phenomenal success. He could no more deal with this request than the Moonie representative could face comfortably the question about the success of the Mormons. Also in that same month of December, we heard theologian Herbert Richardson of the University of Toronto declare the Reverend Moon's book *Divine Principle* to be the most important theological work in the twentieth century. Dr. Richardson was quite serious in claiming that the Reverend Moon and the Unification Church were a genuine manifestation and work of God in our midst. Professor Frederick Sontag, who has completed an extensive study of Sun Myung Moon and the Unification Church, seems unable to decide in his own mind what of the Reverend Moon's work is of God and what is not.[3] Indeed, he seems to take the attitude of Gamaliel in the fifth chapter of Acts: if a religious movement succeeds and thrives, then it must have had divine support and backing. But not even Billy Graham, with his earlier emphasis upon success, would now subscribe to this principle of explanation.

When one of us in January 1979 on KERA-FM, Dallas, interviewed the Texas Director of the Moonies and asked him whether Muhammad had or had not received divine revelation from God, he replied no. Unwilling, however, to conclude that the Qur'an (Koran) of Muhammad was either inspired by Satan or caused by natural and psychological

---

[3]See Frederick Sontag, *Sun Myung Moon and the Unification Church* (Nashville: Abingdon, 1977), pp. 210-16.

conditions alone, the director finally conjectured that the Qur'an had come from the spirit world. This answer gave him freedom to add that the Qur'an is a good religious book even though lacking the authority of the Reverend Moon's *Divine Principle*. As for the Book of Mormon, the Texas Moonie director gave it the same ranking as he gave the Qur'an.

From Billy Graham to the Reverend Moon

The time is ripe for a more thoroughly naturalistic and humanistic approach to the new exotic religions as well as, for example, Billy Graham's evangelical version of Christianity. When we asked the public relations woman of the Unification Church whether she was willing to grant that God had actually spoken to Joseph Smith and had given him an infallible revelation in the form of the Book of Mormon she was unwilling to do so. She even moved toward a naturalistic account of the growth of Mormonism, indicating that it was the work of neither demons nor God. But in the process of suggesting her own naturalistic account of the rise of Mormonism, she began to realize that someone might take the same naturalistic categories and use them to explain the Moonies as well.

To offer a naturalistic framework for gaining insight into the nature and context of religious conversions of various types is not to say that all conversions are cut from one and the same piece of cloth. Naturalism does not require us to say that no evaluation can be made about one style of conversion over another. Indeed, naturalism indicates how such an evaluation might be made with insight.

We believe that the naturalistic framework of this book will offer to many of our readers a significantly new way of looking at the fascinating phenomenon of religious conversion. It is a mark against many of our fellow naturalists, however, that they have too easily dismissed the conversion process and its dynamics. Instead of attempting to look carefully into religious conversion, they have failed to appreciate the significance of some of its most profound structures and underlying conditions.

A Critical Question

Over the past three years we regularly have been receiving reading material from Jerald and Sandra Tanner of Salt Lake City, Utah. They had been faithful Mormons for many years until their conversion to evangelical Christianity. Currently they are working zealously to expose what they regard as serious flaws and contradictions in the Mormon religion. By contrast, just when several faithful Mormons were leaving their faith, a Church of Christ minister was converted to Mormonism in 1967. Those leaving this faith and those coming into it hold one belief in common. Those leaving believe that God is guiding them out. Those coming in believe that God is positively involved in their new conversion.

We referred earlier to a young Moonie who had been an evangelical Lutheran. The young spokesman of the Krishna Consciousness movement in America had been a Methodist. We also met an older Moonie who had been raised as a Presbyterian in Korea. With these observations at hand, we are prompted to raise the question, "Is *any* religious conversion a supernatural work of God, or are they one and all to be explained by naturalistic causes and conditions?"

Billy Graham once said, "At the alarming rate of spiritual decline in the West, it is conceivable that God is getting Koreans ready to serve as missionaries to the Western churches."[4] But it is unlikely that Graham had the Reverend Moon in mind when he made this statement, and he certainly would not regard himself as Moon's forerunner. Even though there are some astounding similarities between Dr. Graham and the Reverend Moon, Graham cannot regard Moon's own dramatic religious conversion to be an authentic and genuine supernatural work of God. In order to account for the Reverend Moon's personal conversion, Dr. Graham's evangelical framework forces him to conclude that Moon's experience was either the work of Satan or the work of natural forces embodied in a social and cultural setting. Our approach will be to account for every conversion—whether Billy Graham's or Sun Myung Moon's—as the product of sociocultural forces in a natural setting.

By moving in and out of several frames of reference over the years, we believe we have improved our own understanding of the "new birth." We therefore would be self-contradictory if we should begrudge our readers the freedom to make use of several frames of reference. The significance of our book over others written on the theme of religious conversion is that we offer a thoroughgoing naturalistic approach without any mixture of supernaturalism. Books on the new birth are many. But a book on this topic written from an exclusively naturalistic framework is both rare and long overdue.

Undergoing Conversion at Several Levels

We now raise the question of whether it is possible to undergo a conversion without realizing that it is happening to oneself. As we will show in a later chapter, there is reason to believe that many people are profoundly converted but do not describe themselves as having been

---

[4]Quoted in Kurt Koch, *Victory Through Persecution* (Grand Rapids: Kregel Publications, 1972).

"born again." Many people who say they are born again do not recognize *subsequent conversion processes* taking place in their own lives.

Billy Graham, for example, gives many indications of currently undergoing at least a minor conversion which could become sweeping in scope if his external conditions, circumstances, and social bonds were to alter significantly. Although such a sweeping change is unlikely, it is nevertheless worth asking the question, "If Dr. Graham should undergo a sweeping conversion, how would he relate to his many evangelical friends, many of whom have been closely associated with him in deep friendship for about four decades?" (The critical role of personal associations in being "born again" will be discussed in a later chapter.)

It is true that Billy Graham has made almost no significant shifts in his basic religious beliefs since he began preaching in the 1940's. That is why his November 1977 interview with a reporter of *McCall's Magazine* is so important. Dr. Graham said frankly and reflectively:

> I used to play God, but I can't do that any more. I used to believe that pagans in far-off countries were lost—were going to hell—if they did not have the gospel of Jesus Christ preached to them. I no longer believe that. I believe that there are other ways of recognizing the existence of God—through nature, for instance—and plenty of other opportunities, therefore, of saying "yes" to God.[5]

This statement surprised many people and deeply disturbed a number of Graham's fellow evangelical Christians. Only a few months before making this startling statement, Graham had written in *How to Be Born Again* that it was cynicism that provoked people to ask, "What about the pagans who have never heard of Jesus?"[6] This quite naturally prompts the question, "Has Billy Graham now become a cynic?" We think not. But something is deeply troubling him. Graham is not a man who gives voice to his doubts about his religious beliefs. Indeed, in times past he has classified doubt under the heading of sin and disloyalty. But there is a serious conflict in this evangelist's belief-value system, and he seems to have become somewhat aware of it and to be wrestling with it. What has brought about this serious conflict within Graham's belief-value system?

Billy Graham has had to face the fierce and threatening question of whether his Jewish friends—of whom he has surprisingly many—must

---

[5]James Michael Beam, "Billy Graham: 'I Can't Play God Anymore'," *McCall's Magazine*, 105: 4 (January, 1978), 157-58.

[6](Waco, Texas: Word Books, 1977), pp. 55-56.

become believers in Jesus as the Messiah and divine Son of God in order to be born again! Dr. Graham has grown uncomfortable with this and closely related questions, and his more recent responses to these questions have proved unsatisfactory to a number of his evangelical friends and associates, including his old friend Bill Bright, head of the Campus Crusade for Christ. Dr. Graham is, of course, bound theologically by the very plain and blunt statement in Acts 4:12 which insists that salvation can be had under no other name than Jesus Christ of Nazareth. Faced both with this uncompromising passage and with his conspicuous desire not to see in hell his Jewish and pagan friends who do not adhere to his version of Jesus as the supernatural Christ, Graham finds himself facing a serious dilemma. Unable to work through it satisfactorily, the evangelist has had to settle with the assertion that while he is "told [by the Bible] to preach Christ as the only way to salvation," he is forced to leave it to God to solve the dilemma, that is, to "do the judging."[7]

When Dr. Graham read his November 1977 interview, he himself was disturbed by what he had said. But unable honestly to deny that he had actually made the controversial statements, he later commented that the statements had not given the *meaning* that he had *intended.* "I do believe that non-Christians are lost—whether they live in far off countries or in America," he said, but went on to affirm "that Jesus Christ is the only way of salvation."[8] The fact seems to be that Billy Graham is torn in two directions. One dimension of his thinking and behavior has been converted in one direction, a direction in conflict with that of his previous conversion. It is important to realize that far from being a simple phenomenon, conversion in one person can often take place at diverse dimensions and in various directions. A *total* conversion of the individual, in which every aspect of his being moves uniformly in one direction, is a mere fiction. In Romans 7 Paul's description of himself as a divided self is much more realistic than the fiction of total conversion. (We will examine Romans 7 in another chapter.)

Because no one's conversion is complete and total in every respect, there lies in every conversion the seeds of either its own undoing or its own self-transcendence. When the less-than-perfect conversion contains at its center a severe dilemma or value-conflict, it faces the possibility of a subsequent conversion that could in some sense disqualify the former

---

[7]Ibid., p. 56.

[8]Quoted in "Dr. Graham: 'I Used to Play God'—New View Change," *The Texas Methodist,* 124: 30 (January 6, 1978), 4.

conversion.* It is useful to understand that the threat of a subsequent conversion replacing the previous one is for some people more likely to take place at an unconscious level—at least for a while, until the new processes and values gain a viable support system of their own.

Accordingly, if Billy Graham eventually stands by his statements made in the November 1977 interview, he will have undergone an *advanced* stage of religious conversion, which would probably be the most important conversion in the life of this evangelist since he first became an evangelist. But how far he will follow through with this conversion in his thinking, in his relating to others, and in his preaching—all this remains to be seen. The more thoroughly he follows the implications of it, the more radical will his recent conversion become. He is already aware of an earlier shift in his theological outlook, and on more than one occasion he has commented on it. It was a shift to a more open attitude toward Christians other than his fellow conservatives. This change to a more inclusive outlook and attitude came about largely by his associating with and working directly with Lutherans, Catholics and other Christians, many of whom helped him in his crusades. We think that his close contact with Jews and other non-Christians has in effect forced Billy Graham to rethink his whole attitude toward his fellow human beings. But this implies in addition a rethinking of the place of Jews and non-Christians in his theological scheme of things.

Dr. Graham recently said that if he were to live his life again, he would preach less and study more. There are signs that he is currently entering a more reflective and contemplative period of his life. It remains to be seen whether his desire to study will be carried out in an environment that gives him an increased independence of thought and mind. As we will show later, religion invariably has a cognitive or intellectual dimension. But this dimension can be seriously retarded if its social and intellectual environment is closed too tightly or fails to provide powerful stimulation and reinforcement. In 1972 one of us wrote a chapter on "Christian Americanism," which was devoted to Dr. Graham's tendency to identify his Christianity with Americanism.[9] Other writers have also called attention to this nationalistic Christianity, and in November 1977 Graham himself stated that in the fifties "I almost

---

*In a recent article historian Richard V. Pierard discussed Graham's recent shifting on war: see Pierard's "Billy Graham and Vietnam: From Cold Warrior to Peacemaker," *Christian Scholar's Review* 10:1 (1980), 37-51.

[9] See Joe E. Barnhart, *The Billy Graham Religion* (Philadelphia: Pilgrim Press, 1972), chapter 12.

identified Americanism with Christianity."[10] A very careful study of Graham's career will show that he has undergone a few minor conversions in his adult life and that the latest one—if it takes root—could prove to be a major conversion, posing a major threat to the belief-system of his evangelical faith.

How Many Changes Make A Conversion?

As humanists, we find Dr. Graham's dilemma to be a vivid example of the conflict between, on the one hand, an individual's warm and personal involvement with fellow human beings of faiths different from his own and, on the other hand, his commitment to a religious tradition that is sometimes inhumane, especially in its doctrine of eternal hell for Jews and other non-Christians. In short, and to oversimplify somewhat, Billy Graham's heart is more inclined toward a humanitarian ideal than his fierce evangelical Christian tradition seems to be.

In November 1980 Billy Graham was 62 years old, and we are tempted to conclude that it is unlikely that he will ever publicly announce that he has undergone a conversion so sweeping as to remove him from evangelical Christianity. Rather, it is more likely that within, say, a few more years he will undergo two or three other minor conversions in his belief-value system that will cause some religiously informed editors and writers to debate the *extent* to which he has deviated from his evangelical framework.

We have looked at evangelist Billy Graham in this chapter for a number of reasons. One of those reasons has been to suggest that the religious conversion process is not an intrinsically mysterious phenomenon beyond all human understanding. We have also attempted to indicate by way of the very concrete case of Dr. Billy Graham how a conversion process might germinate and then spread in a person's life.

But to demystify the account of a conversion process is not to say that it is insignificant or that religious conversion is something that can be eliminated from human life. Far from wishing to eliminate religious conversion from the human scene, we wish to throw light on it in order to make some strides toward freeing it from repressive and destructive attachments. Humanists and naturalists have not only a right to contribute to the understanding and enrichment of religious conversion, but a responsibility to do so.

---

[10]"Billy Graham: 'I Can't Play God Anymore'," 154; R. V. Pierard, "Billy Graham and the U. S. Presidency," *Journal of Church and State*, 22:1 (Winter 1980), 107-27.

Advancing a Theory

In advancing the theory that religious conversion is not a supernatural—divine or demonic—inroad into human life or history, we as naturalists and humanists have to throw open many windows of inquiry. Often there is strong resistance to opening these windows. But it is imperative if we are to increase our understanding and appreciation of religious conversion. Indeed, it would be quite useful to know why converts—whether to Mormonism or to Communism—are sometimes willing to go to great lengths to repress inquiry into the social, psychological, economic, linguistic, and other conditions of their conversion.

Already, by speaking of degrees of conversion and of minor conversions and even of multiple conversions in the individual's life, we have begun to introduce a naturalistic and humanistic bias into our search into the "born again" phenomenon. To some of our readers, our book will appear to open too many doors, too many avenues. This is nonetheless what we insist on doing, for our contention is that the new birth or conversion is a very rich, complex, and complicated process.

Three Dimensions of Religious Conversion

We will close this chapter by reminding our readers that we began our inquiry into religious conversion with the assumption that the human species is incurably religious and that conversion of various sorts, degrees, and consequences is here to stay. To understand it better, and therefore to deal with it more intelligently and sensitively, we will move deeper into our inquiry by restating that religious conversion has at least three major dimensions: (1) the psychological, (2) the social, and (3) the cultural. We turn now to the psychological dimension.

Chapter II

The Psychological Dimension of the Second Birth

The Importance and Limits of the Psychological Approach

If an art critic were to go with his students to an art gallery to help them to understand and appreciate more fully some of the great works of art, he might begin by asking them to focus exclusively on the lines within the painting. He would speak of the complex relationships between the lines, and the "structure" of the painting. There would be certain patterns, connections, and even problems of configuration which the artist seemed to be wrestling with in his work. Only later would the art critic shift his students' attention from the lines per se in order to focus exclusively on the colors within the painting. The "play of colors" could then become itself a distinct subject of inquiry. What was the artist doing with this color, this shade rather than another? How does this orange relate to this gray? And so on.

Yet no one knows better than the art critic that not only is the painting all these various parts and distinct emphases, but it is also a *whole* creation. The same may be said of religious conversion and the new birth. It can be looked at as a psychological phenomenon. But it is not exclusively psychological, just as a painting is not exclusively the lines and configurations. There is the social dimension of religious conversion as well. There are also the cultural or philosophical dimensions. The religious new birth is not one of these in exclusion of the others, but it is the whole of them in their very special interrelationship.

To say that a painting is a *whole* creation is not to say that it is an unintelligible glob or blur. Its wholeness lies not in ignoring the lines and colors, but in drawing them into focus and placing them in their perspective and interrelationship with one another and with the other dimensions of the painting. Similarly, the new birth is no mere glob of mystery. It is a system of complex and fascinating interrelationships of psychological, social, cultural, or philosophical dimensions. At the psychological level, religious conversion may be seen as a response to the individual's sense of either his personal condition of finiteness or the finiteness of whatever gives him his fundamental identity. We advance the general thesis that *at the psychological level, religion is first and foremost the anxious concern with, or sense of, one's own finitude.*

The Sense of Finitude

Psychiatrists generally agree that one of the most crushing experiences that can befall a human child is the feeling that his parents have abandoned him or will abandon him. There is a very moving verse in one of the Psalms which reads, "When my mother and my father forsake me, then the Lord will take me up" (Psalms 28:10 KJV). This is in many ways the starting point of every religion—to find a way to come to terms with the threat of the absolute and ultimate loss of all supports essential for meaningful human existence. We call this the *concern with finitude.* This concern—this incurable preoccupation—emerges when the individual through one experience or another comes to sense his finitude, that is, his inescapable position of dependency and his condition of always being a limited creature.

J. Milton Yinger notes in *The Scientific Study of Religion,* "Death is the most difficult and serious problem with which religion attempts to deal."[1] This is true because there is nothing like the fact of death in the world to remind human creatures of their creatureliness and their ultimate finitude. Death has of course social and even political and economic consequences. But the process of personally facing one's own eventual death and that of one's dearest friends and relatives is clearly a psychological phenomenon having far-reaching consequences.

Religious conversion—the new birth or being "born again"—is fundamentally a response to this sense of human finitude. The individual senses and feels the finitude of either his own individual self or his primary identity group. (In some tribal cultures, personal identity is not

---

[1](New York: Macmillan Co., 1970),p. 126.

singled out in sharp contrast to the basic identity group.) This sense of ultimate helplessness is the rock-bottom problem and concern of religion. While we do not agree with those who claim that all religions are heading in the same direction, we do contend that they are above all else endeavoring to come to terms with the pervasive and perennial sense of absolute dependency, impermanence, and limitation. This can be seen in the way various religions have attempted to deal with "the destroying action of Time."[2] Some have flatly denied that time is a reality at all. It is mere illusion. Others have portrayed time as a temporary interlude somehow within the spread of eternity. Others have looked upon time as something like crests of waves upon which the fortunate could ride without being lost in the storm. Time itself is swallowed up in victory, so the promise goes.

Every finite individual is dependent in thousands of ways on his physical, social, and cultural environment. Within limits, it may be a relative matter as to which particular form of society or culture he depends on, but it is not a relative matter that he is dependent absolutely on some society and culture if he is to be a vital human person. And of course all peoples everywhere depend on nature for existence. Our point here is this: when the structure of this pervasive dependency is threatened or disturbed, the individual becomes aware of the finitude of himself or his basic identity group. That is, he feels the threat of a certain final and absolute helplessness. Relatively speaking, the individual is not helpless. But this is true only insofar as the underlying physical, social, and cultural structures hold together. In a more ultimate sense, the individual is literally helpless; for if the underlying structures are taken away, he literally cannot help himself. He is absolutely helpless under those dire conditions.

This sense of finitude may "hit" a child with a profound and far-reaching impact when one of his parents dies, for a parent is usually a significant part of the child's physical and social environment. It is therefore not surprising that some religions reach out for an eternal Father or Mother who will not die. Nor is it surprising that most religions long for a kind of utopian social and physical environment wherein famine, disease, hostilities, death, and agony are not to be found.

Deborah Morgan, age 28, married at the age of 27 for the first time. During the same year she became an evangelical Christian. "I was desperate," she explained. "I had just left a man whom I had lived with for five years. I'm a chemical-dependent person." Deborah is still

---

[2]Mircea Eliade, *Rites and Symbols of Initiation*, p. 136.

dependent on speed, caffein tablets, and marijuana. Her conversion to evangelicalism was obviously an attempt to find a lasting cure of the curse of finitude. She had, as it were, looked into the abyss to discover that her entire finite life could easily come to naught.

The Moral Mode of Finitude

There are at least three modes in which the sense of rock-bottom finitude manifests itself. They are (1) the moral, (2) the emotional, and (3) the intellectual or cognitive.

Those individuals and groups who suffer their finitude in the mode of *morality* will regard themselves as living under a burden of *guilt*. Of course, every socialized individual feels guilty at times. But guilt becomes religious in quality when the individual senses that he is helpless in himself alone to remove the guilt. To be guilty is to stand in a special kind of relationship with some other being—human or otherwise. The individual who resorts to power alone to remove the guilt may in the process discover his finitude in another way. He may discover that in resorting to power to remove guilt, he has destroyed a relationship of another kind, one which he wants or perhaps needs desperately.

The nineteenth century theologian Friedrich Schleiermacher regarded religion in its most preliminary and pervasive form to be the sense of *absolute dependency*. To be really guilty (rather than merely to feel guilty) is to be dependent on at least the wronged person's offer to restore the disturbed relationship. The recognition of one's guilt takes on a religious quality when the guilty person understands that the use of his power and manipulation alone will not remove his guilt. In short, he is helpless—without power—to eliminate his own guilt. He is *absolutely dependent* on the other person to forgive and thus remove the burden of guilt.

But there are cases in which the individual who was wronged will not forgive. What does the guilty person do in such a situation? He is truly repentant, but still forgiveness does not come. At this point, the community may enter the picture to negotiate the forgiveness. It may be that the wronged individual is himself using his power to manipulate the guilty party. The community—or an objective agent of the community—may step in to pass judgment. Doubtless, in many communities, the image of a deity has functioned as a kind of independent, objective court of appeal. The guilty person may feel that he is absolutely dependent on the deity or on the community to extend forgiveness and acceptance. However, many religions have deities that have their own narrow vested interests and power plays. In concrete terms, this means that those who claim to be the spokesmen of such deities gain a certain power of manipulation for themselves.

The individual who senses his finitude in the mode of morality will feel that he has in some way *betrayed or violated* some standard or expectations which he ought to have lived up to. Passing judgment on himself, he confesses that he has wronged someone or betrayed the moral code, the community, or the deity. He may even suffer a kind of *finitude-shock* when he looks back and sees the evil that he has done. Sometime after being convicted in Judge Sirica's court, Charles Colson wrote, "How calloused I'd been all those past years about the importance of one individual's rights."[3]

If the individual feels that he was deeply involved in betraying the moral code, the community or the deity, then he may come to see himself as justly *alienated*—a moral outcast. He sees himself as having died morally, as having become incurably disloyal, and now in a hopeless and helpless condition. Something outside himself must rescue him, save him from the quicksand of betrayal in which he has involved himself. In short, as he stands now—defiled, unclean, morally dead—he must somehow become *another person*. He must be born again. But when he realizes that it is not in his power alone to do this, then at that point he moves into the religious dimension of human experience.

The realization that he had betrayed his identity group—his country—descended slowly but steadily on Charles W. Colson, who was Richard Nixon's "hatchet man." Here are his own words:

> It wasn't the United States against me, I wanted to cry out, it was a group of politicized individuals. My own country was not accusing me—but of course it was. That frightful realization, which until this very moment I resisted, brought a feeling of nausea. Nothing that could be done to me—trials, prison, ruin—nothing would match the dreadful knowledge that the country I loved was charging me with a breach of my trust and duty.[4]

Colson came to believe that he, a man who had served in high and powerful positions, had become a moral alien to his own community. Eventually, he found a way to gain acceptance, to be restored to the community; but the process was not easy. He came to describe himself as having been "born again." Despite his time in prison and the agony and

---

[3]Charles W. Colson, *Born Again* (New York: Bantam Press, 1976), p. 236.

[4]Ibid., p. 235.

humiliation suffered after realizing that he had indeed violated the sacred trust of the community, Colson was nevertheless a very fortunate man. In time, he did become accepted as a "babe in Christ" by a very large number of influential Christians, and today he enjoys considerable fame as a superstar convert to the evangelical Christian faith.

· But not every society can forgive every sin. Perhaps every society has some "unpardonable sin." Consider the following:

> In ancient Bali, the punishment [for incest] was symbolic and devastating. The hapless couple were adorned with yokes customarily worn by pigs. They were then made to crawl on all fours to drink from the swill trough of the hogs. After this humiliation, they were banished forever from the village, and their lands were confiscated. No other village would take them in for fear of ill luck and disaster. They were doomed to a fearsome existence alone in the jungle.[5]

To experience one's finitude in the mode of morality is to walk in dread of ultimate and final banishment from *any* decent community. It is to be a man or woman, boy or girl, who finally does not belong. Or if he does belong, it is to a group that he can neither respect nor cherish. Indeed, to be *identified with* moral outcasts is to suffer nothing less than a severe *identity crisis*. Colson could not bear the thought of having his own personal identity defined and sealed in terms of criminals, thugs, and underworld characters. He wrote:

> Inside the small plain-walled probation office, . . . I began to feel the reality of what it was to be a convicted felon. Here a clerk would write up my report just as he did each day for street criminals, rapists, car thieves, and narcotics peddlers. I had put myself here . . . I would now be in the hands of GS-7 probation clerks, marshals, prison guards. The loss of control of my body and life was a sensation I had not fully understood before.[6]

Even before his conviction, Colson found himself sneaking in and out of buildings, rumpled hat over his eyes, and glancing from side to side. He wondered whether he would get adjusted to the ways of the criminal world.[7] He could not adjust to or live with the image of the man that he saw himself to be. He had to become a new person, born anew. (Later, in

---

[5]E. Adamson Hoebel, *Anthropology: The Study of Man*, 3rd ed., (New York: McGraw-Hill Book Co., 1958), p. 338.

[6]Colson, *Born Again*, p. 266.

[7]See ibid., p. 230.

Chapter 6, we will deal with the question of genuine conversion in contrast to pseudo-conversion.)

The Emotional Mode of Finitude

A divorce counselor in Dallas once asked us to observe one of her group counseling sessions so that we could later give her our evaluations of her performance as a counselor. We were struck at once by the fact that the members of the group were hurting very much. On our left was a radio talk-show host who had only recently gone through a divorce. Despite the fact that he was a burly individual with a good measure of fame and position, the man was obviously experiencing an emotional crisis. He could not praise the group enough for working with him in his crisis.

The second thing that struck us about the group was the constant emphasis upon the importance of "being independent"—"being on your own." But our third observation was that despite the talk of independence, the group members were in fact quite *emotionally dependent* on their counselor and on one another. We saw this as a realistic dependency relationship, since they were also making plans for finding other reinforcers and supports to be utilized after the termination of the counseling sessions.

In the process of living year by year, people are reminded now and then that all of their meaningful human relationships will eventually perish either wholly or in significant aspects. The emotional impact of this loss can sometimes be so overwhelming that the individual becomes quite vulnerable. There are also other losses—of limb, job, looks, teeth, abilities that once could be taken for granted, confidence, memory, and so forth. Such losses can sometimes extract a considerable emotional toll when they remind the individual that it is possible for him to lose everything.

Harold Hughes came face to face with his finitude when he discovered that in himself alone he was powerless to cope with the hold that alcohol had on his life. "Defeated," "weak," "undone," "empty," "lonely"—these are a few of the words that have been used to express the individual's finitude when experienced in the mode of human *emotion*. Harold Hughes was fortunate to have been transformed from a barroom brawler and an irresponsible drunk to eventually a very responsible and informed senator from Iowa. Having reached his rope's end as a drunk, he seriously contemplated suicide. Unable to function in a way that gave him self-respect, he had to face the bitter truth that his life was a wreck, a disaster. This tough, brawling truck driver came to realize that he had lost every battle with the bottle. The consequence of realizing that he was a defeated man proved to be nothing less than a religious crisis at the psychological level, especially the emotional level.

The stories of Sakyamuni (who later became Buddha) reveal a young prince in northern India who at the age of nineteen had most of what many people spend all of their lives striving to gain. And yet, so the stories go, Sakyamuni was converted from this favored way of life to a wholly different and more difficult way: "According to Buddhist tradition, it is believed that he realized the impermanence of this world on the occasion of his seeing an old man, a sick person and a corpse."[8]

Whether or not these experiences are precisely what transformed young Sakyamuni is not so important as the fact that the ancient Buddhist tradition focused on the heart of the religious problem—the problem of the finitude of everything. For centuries, Buddhists have called attention to the impermanence and interdependency of everything. The realization of the impermanence of all earthly things is the starting point of Buddhism and every other religion. One Hebrew prophet wrote:

> All flesh is grass, and all its beauty is like the flower of the
> field. The grass withers, the flower fades, when the breath of
> the Lord blows upon it; surely the people is grass (Isaiah 40:6-
> 7 RSV).

A person need not feel guilty or even woefully ignorant just to sense emotionally the impermanence and finitude of either himself or the very structures of existence. He quite naturally raises the question of whether there is *anything* permanent and enduring. In raising such a question, he is showing himself to be religious to the extent that the question rose out of a profound concern over the appearance of finitude at every turn.

The Intellectual Mode of Finitude

Just after Vatican II had begun to stir Roman Catholics everywhere, we heard a devout Catholic exclaim, "What does it all mean; what's it add up to? I can't make sense of the Church any more." Every religious faith entails beliefs, that is, statements that purport to be true. Children grow up in communities which impart to them a system of beliefs or doctrines. For various reasons, some individuals are able to see contradictions and serious problems in their inherited belief system. When they sense the far-reaching implications of the imperfection of their belief-system, they may become desperate to find a perfect system, or if not perfect, then the best one among the rivals.

---

[8]Shoyu Hanayama, "Buddhism," in R. C. Chalmers and John A. Irving, eds., *The Meaning of Life in Five Great Religions* (Philadelphia: Westminster Press, 1965), p. 39.

When suffering the realization that his cherished belief-system contains very critical self-contradictions, a person may be said to be experiencing the sense of finitude in the intellectual or cognitive mode. Those who do not experience the depths of their finitude in this way seldom appreciate the desperation of the sufferer to find a more coherent and satisfactory belief-system. If the sufferer comes to think that he has indeed found the ideal belief-system, the joy that touches him is almost beyond compare. Arthur Koestler knew this feeling of joy or rapture. He wrote:

> To say that one had "seen the light" is a poor description of the mental rapture which only the convert knows (regardless of what faith he has been converted to). The new light seems to pour in from all directions across the skull; the whole universe falls into pattern like the stray pieces of a jigsaw puzzle assembled by magic at one stroke. There is now an answer to every question, doubts and conflicts are a matter of the tortured past—a past already remote, when one had lived in dismal ignorance in the tasteless, colorless world of those who *don't know.*[9]

Koestler, who had once experienced a moving and dramatic conversion to Communism, told of a Communist writer who "knew his Marx and Lenin backwards and forwards and had that absolute, serene faith which exerts a hypnotic power over other people's minds."[10] We ourselves have known quite a few evangelical and fundamentalist Christians who could quote Scripture with the fierce conviction that they were serving divine truths hot off the altar of God. When he was a loyal and faithful Marxist, ready to go where the Party wanted him to go, Koestler simply worked from the assumption that "both morally and logically the Party was infallible."[11]

The Craving for Infallibility

How is it that men and women can come to believe that they have a document of some sort or a Party that is an infallible source of truth? Millions of pious Muslims hold the Qur'an (Koran) to be the infallible, unerring revelation of the one and only true God. Evangelicals and

---

[9]Arthur Koestler, "The Initiates," in Richard Crossman, ed., *The God That Failed* (New York: Bantam Books, 1952), p. 19.

[10]Ibid., p. 20.

[11]Ibid., p. 29.

fundamentalists among Christians insist that the Bible (in its original autographs) is divine truth "without mixture of error." Recently, the evangelical Biblical scholar Dewey M. Beegle in his book *Scripture, Tradition, and Infallibility* created quite a controversy among the faithful when he wrote that, while the Bible is indeed the revelation of God, it contains just a slight measure of error—"minor historical errors," he explained.[12]

Opponents to Professor Beegle's concession were quick to point out that to admit that there was even one flaw, one error, in the original documents of the Bible is to open the door for all sorts of questions to be raised about flaws and errors in *every part* of the Bible. There is a point to this reply. Unfortunately, it does nothing to refute Beegle's claim that there are some errors in the Bible. Instead, it says that the consequences of admitting errors could be worse for evangelical Christianity than Beegle seems to have realized.

To be sure, evangelicals have offered some positive arguments in an attempt to defend the view that the Bible is the infallible or inerrant revelation of God. But Muslims have argued equally well for the Qur'an's trustworthiness as God's unerring revelation. Of course, Christians are not accustomed to taking seriously any claim that the religion of Islam is in fact the true religion. In his provocative article "Why Not Islam?" R. C. Zaehner points out that when some of the Jewish leaders were about to write off Christianity, an esteemed Jewish teacher of the Law named Gamaliel told his fellow Jews to leave the Christians alone. His reasoning was as follows: If their new movement is of God, then no one will be able to put them down. Gamaliel even warned: "You might even be found opposing God." Zaehner adds, "No one has so far succeeded in putting the Muslims down." Are Muslims then perhaps from God?[13]

Our point here is that numerous arguments have been used in the attempt to prop up the doctrine of an infallible revelation. Many of the arguments seem unworthy of human intelligence, and yet sincere men and women embrace them with a certain desperation. To suggest that the *survival* of Christianity or Islam over the centuries might at least serve as evidence for the divine approval of one of them raises all sorts of comical questions. Does the cockroach have divine sanction? Does it perhaps have apostolic succession? The survival of the cockroach through all sorts

---

[12](Grand Rapids: Eerdmans, 1973), p. 276.

[13]See R. C. Zaehner, "Why Not Islam?" *Religious Studies*, 11:2 (June 1975), 179.

of opposition makes the survival of the Bible or Qur'an seem a modest achievement to say the least. So, why do sincere and earnest people continue obsessively to attempt to prop up the doctrine of an inerrant, infallible document?

The religious motive in the craving for an infallible document is not difficult to understand. If people already believe that there is a God requiring them to make a choice regarding their "eternal destiny," they quite naturally will wonder whether this God has given any reliable directions about what the options are and what the steps are in helping people to make the wisest choice, especially since the choice is so absolutely crucial in its consequences.

Also in their desire for both moral and intellectual orientation, many people find it quite natural to ask whether some "map" or document exists to provide this orientation. Indeed, some people insist that without such a document, the only alternative is chaos. Clark Pinnock, in his *Biblical Revelation: The Foundation of Christian Theology,* expresses this position with obvious alarm:

> Modern theology of almost every shade is in crisis. While there is no lack of religious verbosity, a sure word resonant with divine authority is scarcely to be heard ... Contemporary theology has become relativistic and hesitating. The gravity of the crisis for the churches should not be underestimated. The foundations have been shaken.[14]

Pinnock goes on to add that the question of the authority of the Bible as infallible revelation from heaven is *the central problem* for theology. "Everything hangs on our solution to it."[15] He speaks of the desperate need to provide "our searching generation with *a map to lead them out of the tangle of modern theological confusion.*"[16]

There are of course a number of documents and traditions which claim to provide an unerring revelation of truth about what the cosmos is like, in general outline at least, and what is morally required of everyone. Unfortunately, there seems to be no infallible guide that will show people which—if any—of the putative revelations is the genuine one. Some Christians contend that the Holy Spirit as an "inner witness" is the perfect compass guiding the sincere seeker to the one and only reliable Scripture. But there is now, and always has been, a controversy as to who really has the Spirit—is it the Charismatics, the Lutherans, the Hare

---

[14](Chicago: Moody Press, 1971), p. 9.

[15]Ibid., p. 11. Italics added.

[16]Ibid., p. 10. Italics added.

Krishnas, or one of the many others who speak of the Holy Spirit? Of course, this controversy is built on the metaphysical assumption that there is a divine Holy Spirit in the first place who somehow guides people's choices.

The Paradox of Psychology of Religion

There is a paradox in the study of religion from the psychological perspective. The study keeps reaching beyond the circle of psychology and into metaphysics. An individual person is not a pigeon who reacts exclusively to flashes of lights or to sounds of bells. There is also the complex cognitive or intellectual environment to which he responds. And to have a profound understanding of a person's religious responses and conversion, we must ourselves become familiar with some of the cognitive or intellectual environment of that religion. In short, we must see a religious conversion against the background of the convert's belief-system or his metaphysical framework.

We turn now to consider two conversions or rebirth experiences that were of historical significance. The first is John Henry Newman's conversion to Roman Catholicism. The second is the conversion of Ernest Renan from Roman Catholicism to Humanism. We will also consider in passing the famous conversion of John Wesley, founder of the Methodist movement. We wish to point out how each of these individuals came to terms with his inherited assumption of an infallible revelation from God. How did this assumption work itself out in their fascinating lives? Our purpose in the remainder of this chapter is to provide a measure of historical perspective to the contemporary interest in religious conversion.

The Case of John Henry Newman

As a minister of the Church of England, John Henry Newman (1801-1890) had witnessed Roman Catholics converting to the Anglican faith. But on October 8, 1845, he came to realize fully that he was experiencing his own conversion from the Anglican faith to Roman Catholicism. Nineteen years later he would write in his famous *Apologia pro Vita Sua* that since converting to his new faith, he has enjoyed "perfect peace and contentment" and has "never had one doubt."[17] In this chapter we will discuss Ernest Renan, who could no longer find peace within the Roman Catholic faith because he was increasingly plagued by doubts about the

---

[17](Garden City, N.Y.: Image Books, Doubleday, 1956), p. 317.

truth of this faith. Both Newman and Renan assumed that if God were to reveal his saving truth to mankind, this truth would have to be revealed infallibly—that is, without error or flaw.

The Question of Authority

At the age of fifteen, John Henry Newman experienced a significant change in his outlook. He was moved by the thought that a person must have something firm and fixed to believe in if he is to avoid being carried about as a leaf in the wind.[18] Behind this thought was the conviction that the fundamental interest of all interests is that of the relationship between God and the soul. All other interests were, for Newman, regarded as comparatively insignificant. Our concern in this chapter is not to determine whether Newman's metaphysical assumption was or was not rooted in reality. Here we cannot even delve into the question of whether there is or is not a soul or a God. Rather, in this chapter we want to gain some insight into the psychology of conversion—or the new birth process.

In order to enjoy certainty regarding his soul's status before God, young Newman faced the question of the *authority* for determining the right way to approach God. This issue of authority became increasingly central to Newman's entire adult life. For many years, he had believed that the Anglican Church was the most reliable religious authority and earthly overseer of God's revelation. But doubts kept creeping in under the door. The more he studied Church history and theology, the more he came to question whether the Church of England was in fact the rock on which Christ had built his church. Liberalism in the Church of England frightened him because it seemed to him to lack authority. Also Newman was disturbed that two-thirds of the nation had given up going to church. Furthermore, only one-third of the population was Anglican, the rest being non-conformists.

Newman looked upon non-conformists such as Baptists, Quakers, Presbyterians and the like as having one major flaw in common with religious liberalism—they lacked authority. To be sure, many non-conformists insisted that they had an authority—the infallible Bible—on which to build their faith. But Newman was disturbed by the fact that so many divirgent interpretations and so many bitter disputes could still break out among those who accepted the Bible as their final authority.

It was a part of Newman's psychological makeup to demand a very special kind of authority—one that would provide an unerring

---

[18]See ibid., pp. 127-29.

interpretation or system of interpretations. What good was the Bible as an authority if endless disputes arose about how to interpret it and apply it? Newman's personal psychological structure required some final voice to settle the disputes and to hand down the unquestioned, infallible verdict. Slowly but steadily, he moved toward the conclusion that the Church of Rome was the final interpreter of God's will and doctrine for mankind.

There is little doubt that Newman experienced a conversion or a new birth. Whether or not it was an authentic conversion philosophically or metaphysically is of course a matter of debate. But the point here is that he did undergo a significant conversion that had the characteristics of a profound psychological transformation. For many years he had been hounded by the question of what the core of the Christian faith is. The more he tried to reconcile his Anglican faith with his attractions to Rome, the more he suffered severe ambivalence and indecision. To be sure, indecision is something that virtually everyone lives with in various areas of his life. But for Newman, indecision about the true authority of the Christian faith was not something that he could simply adjust to. The issue was too crucial, the stakes too high.

Newman tried to clarify his beliefs about God, the soul, the means of salvation, and about what is required of mankind morally. For him, all these beliefs made an everlasting difference to the individual. That is precisely why he felt he had to resolve the question of the true and authoritative representative of God on earth. If mankind is without such an authority, then could anyone have a clear and certain knowledge of the ways of God, the soul, salvation or morality? Regarding his indecisiveness before converting to Roman Catholicism, he wrote:

> Alas! It was my position for whole years to remain without any satisfactory basis for my religious profession, a state of moral sickness, neither able to acquiesce in Anglicanism, nor able to go to Rome.[19]

This state of mind stands in contrast to his state of mind after his conversion, when he had no more doubt but enjoyed perfect peace. While continuing to think and write on theological topics, he saw himself as having "no changes [in his thinking] to record, and . . . no anxiety of heart whatsoever."[20] He had undergone a radical psychological conversion at the very least. After his conversion, Newman was appointed to a number

---

[19]Ibid., pp. 177-78.

[20]Ibid., p. 317.

of important positions in the Roman Catholic Church and eventually was appointed to serve as a Cardinal of the Church.

The Psychological States of John Henry Newman and John Wesley

A number of lessons can be learned from the study of Newman's conversion. One of these lessons may be looked at briefly by simply asking two questions: First, what can be made of the fact that a person is transformed from one psychological state to another? Second, and more specifically, should a person's radical movement from a state of indecision to peace and contentment count as evidence for the *truth* of the convert's new beliefs? If the answer to this second question is "Yes," then should we conclude that John Henry Newman's new peace and contentment counts as evidence in support of his belief in the supreme authority of the Roman Catholic Church? We recall that Newman claimed that this Church was the spokesman of God on earth especially in matters of religious belief and moral practice.

However, a strictly psychological study of conversion (or the experience of the new birth) reveals that peace and contentment are states of mind enjoyed by *many people of many religious persuasions.* Indeed, a hundred years before Newman's conversion, another famous Anglican minister experienced a conversion that led him in a direction opposite to that which Newman took. This minister, John Wesley (1703-1791), wrote of how in May 1738 in London he was listening to someone read a passage from Martin Luther's *Epistle to the Romans,* when, according to Wesley, "I felt my heart strangely warmed."[21] He added later: "I have constant peace; not one uneasy thought."[22] He even came to feel that he had been freed from all unholy desires.[23]

Even though we will not dwell on the fascinating details of Wesley's conversion, we do wish to call attention to the fact that he had been led to his conversion through the direct influence of a group of Moravian Christians. These Christians held firmly to the conviction that their church was "so led by the Spirit that it was not possible for it to err in anything."[24] Such a claim was regarded by Wesley to be outlandish, and in a candid but generous manner he outlined for them why he could not

---

[21]John Wesley, *The Journal of the Rev. John Wesley, A.M.,* ed. Nehemiah Curnock (London: The Epworth Press, 1938), 1:472.

[22]Ibid., p. 481.

[23]See ibid.

[24]Ibid., p. 494.

agree with them on this point of their doctrine. It is noteworthy that John Henry Newman thought his particular Church was divinely protected from error in all the important matters of religious doctrine and moral pronouncement. Even though Wesley gained peace and joy in his life, as did Newman and the Moravians, he did not regard his new psychological condition to be evidence in support of the theory of an infallible and unerring Church. For Wesley, the truth of a religious claim had to be rooted in a double authority, namely the Bible and the religious experience itself, since the Bible, not the Church, was the deposit of infallible revelations of the divine mind.

The Storm Over Papal Infallibility

As we noted earlier, Newman was severely perplexed over the conspicuous fact that a thicket of controversy had grown up regarding the proper interpretation of the Sacred Scriptures. He came to believe that unless there was an infallible Church to interpret the Scriptures properly, no one could be certain as to which interpretations were or were not credible. But this raised the question of how anyone could be certain that the Roman Catholic Church—or any other Church—is the true representative of God on earth to interpret the Scriptures authoritatively. Newman devoted many of his adult years to answering this thorny question.

To be sure, there were serious questions that fell across his path after his conversion. Some of his critics charged that while the questions were themselves serious, Newman failed to take them seriously. Be that as it may, we think it worth noting that he was an active Roman Catholic during the stormy time when the issue of the infallibility of the pope was being debated heatedly among Catholics. The dogma of Papal Infallibility did not exist until 1870, when it was proclaimed by the Vatican Council. As a loyal Roman Catholic, Newman had fought the move to adopt this dogma, but he lost the battle in 1870. When the dogma of Papal Infallibility was established and made an official part of Roman Catholic faith, Newman's opposition to it ceased at once and completely. He simply accepted it and declared that his former opinions regarding the dogma were unwarranted even though well motivated.[25] Twenty-five years earlier he had committed himself to the belief that the Roman Catholic Church could not err in matters of religious doctrine. And now the Church had itself proclaimed the pope to be infallible. Newman now

---

[25]See Wilfred Ward, *The Life of John Henry Cardinal Newman* (London: Longmans, Green, 1927), 2:234.

faced a painful dilemma. But by committing himself more thoroughly to the premises of his earlier conversion to Roman Catholicism, he was able to embrace the dogma which he had tried earlier to prevent being accepted by his Church.

There were still other apparent difficulties which Newman as a Roman Catholic was forced to deal with. For example, his Church had made claims about such matters as post-biblical miracles, the body of St. Peter, the Crib of Bethlehem, pieces of the cross, the moving eyes of Madonna in the Roman States, and St. Walburga's medicinal oil. Newman's responses to these embarrassments were not very convincing to outsiders. But for him, these difficulties were insignificant when compared to the difficulties that he thought would break out if the infallible authority of the Roman Catholic Church was undermined.[26]

The Background of Theories and Presuppositions

Another insight which the study of John Henry Newman's transformation offers us has to do with the role that theories or presuppositions play in religious experience. Sometimes converts talk as if religious exprience simply happens out of the blue, with no theoretical background or cognitive frame of reference to give it shape and substance. Indeed, in contemporary times, much talk still goes on about "feelings," as if feelings were somehow pure elements removed entirely from the background of beliefs and theories.[27]

It is quite often advisable to admit and celebrate our feelings about something or someone. To admit that we have these feelings is one thing; but to regard our feelings and experiences as unerringly true in their *claims* is quite another thing. Most of our feelings exist against a background of presuppositions and theories. We stress this elementary point in order to say that our background of presuppositions and theories may or may not be warranted in what it asserts. This point has a profound impact on the study of religious conversion, as we will show shortly.

John Wesley insisted that the Bible alone is the infallible revelation of Christian truth, whereas Cardinal Newman regarded the Church to be the infallible voice of Christian truth on earth. What these two men had in common was *the presumption of infallibility* as a part of their theoretical background. The very *structure of the personalities* of these

---

[26]See Radoslav A. Tsanoff, *Autobiographies of Ten Religious Leaders: Alternatives in Christian Experience* (San Antonio: Trinity University Press, 1968), pp. 164-65.

[27]Luke Rhinehart, *The Book of est* (New York: Holt, Rinehart and Winston, 1976), p. 134.

two men was considerably determined by the presumption or assumption that an infallible deposit of truth for human beings was not only possible but required. Had they not had this philosophical presupposition as a part of their background, it is quite possible that many of their other beliefs, attitudes, and decisions would have been different from what they were.

We turn now to the case of Ernest Renan, who, like Newman and Wesley, worked and lived under the presupposition of infallibility. That is, he did so until his religious conversion, which entailed giving up the theoretical presupposition of either an infallible Church or an infallible Scripture. Two days before Newman in England left Anglicanism to become a Roman Catholic, Ernest Renan in France finally decided that he could no longer in good conscience wear the priestly attire of the Roman Catholic Church.

The New Birth of Ernest Renan

Like his contemporary John Henry Newman, Ernest Renan (1823-1892) came early to believe that if a religious faith is worthy of commitment, it must be based on a self-consistent foundation that is free of error. Brought up in the Roman Catholic Church and trained to serve as a priest, Renan dedicated himself to the study of theology. Because he regarded the Bible as the primary and unerring source of Christian teaching and theology, he set out to master the languages of the Bible— Hebrew and Greek. Here Renan and Newman differed in their experiences. Newman never became the Biblical scholar of Renan's stature. Nor was Newman versed in the important Biblical studies going on in Germany in the nineteenth century. The German "higher critics," far from setting out to overturn the Christian faith, were largely Christians who believed that honest critical inquiry should not be suppressed even in the study of the Bible. Religious faith is often a risky business, for it may entail putting the doctrines and assumptions of that faith to test. Renan and many of the German Biblical scholars had committed themselves to testing and gaining a better understanding of the Biblical foundations of their Christian faith.

As a faithful and sensitive Catholic, Renan sought to find the authoritative foundations on which the Christian faith rested. Like Newman, he believed that God had ordained the Roman Catholic Church to be the flawless interpreter of the Sacred Scriptures. But, for Renan, this meant that the Scriptures themselves had to be the primary and flawless revelation of God. To expect to have an infallible interpretation of a Bible that is not itself infallible seemed to Renan to be like expecting to erect a tall and sturdy building on a foundation of mud and quicksand. For him, the Bible had to be taken as unerring in its teachings and claims if the claims of Christian theology were to remain credible.

As an informed Biblical scholar still within the Church, Renan felt the awesome responsibility of delving deeper into the texts of Holy Writ and bringing to light their sacred meaning. To be sure, he did not bear this responsibility alone, for there were other Catholic scholars, too, who were a part of the wider community of Biblical scholars. But Renan became clearly one of Europe's most remarkable researchers in Biblical studies. He received the distinguished appointment to the professorship of Hebrew at the Collège de France. His knowledge of Semitic languages soon became evident to those prominent in the field.

As a young man, he had been encouraged to compete for an academic prize in the field of comparative languages. Accepting the challenge, he completed and submitted his *Historical and Critical Essay on the Semitic Languages in General and on the Hebrew Language in Particular.* The distinguished judges of the contest agreed unanimously that the award should go to Ernest Renan.

In time, he came to be recognized as the foremost master of Hebrew in his native France. But the more his learning as a Biblical scholar increased, the less was he able to believe in Roman Catholic Christianity. Furthermore, the option of evangelical Protestant Christianity was not open to him, for this option also subscribed to the presumption of an infallible Bible. To be sure, this presumption was one which Renan had himself once embraced, but he believed that his Biblical studies and research had forced him to abandon the presumption as unwarranted and unsupportable.[28]

The Old Faith and the New

If Renan's Biblical studies compelled him to leave the faith that he had once dedicated himself to serve as a priest and scholar, the same studies opened up for him a new faith. No longer able to worship Jesus Christ as the divine Savior from heaven, Renan was profoundly moved by what he took to be the vital experience of God which the human Jesus had enjoyed. In that sense, God was in Christ. And Christ was regarded by Renan to be the supreme mediator between God and man.

Renan's own religious journey and his devoted research in Biblical studies led him to give up the following: belief in Jesus as the incarnation of God on earth, belief in the Bible as the infallible revelation of God, and

---

[28]See Radoslav A. Tsanoff, *Autobiographies of Ten Religious Leaders*, pp. 191-198.

belief in the Roman Catholic Church as the unerring interpreter of the Bible. Emotionally, it had been very painful and even agonizing for this learned man to leave behind his Catholic faith. Indeed, he once wrote, "Catholicism satisfies all my faculties, except my critical reason."[29] Many of his dearest friends and former teachers as well as his kind mother were faithful Catholics, but he could not embrace this faith merely because it was their faith.

It would be erroneous to suppose that Ernest Renan was nothing but an intellectual. He had been a devout and active Catholic Christian who prayed, confessed, and sought earnestly to trust and obey the will of God as he had understood it. But his Catholic faith had failed the tests for him. Renan bemoaned the fact that his desperate search through prayer had proved to be a dead-end. It seemed to him that each day another stitch in the fabric of his Catholic faith had broken.

Gradually this sensitive priest came to feel that he should no longer wear the priestly robe, since he was no longer in sufficient agreement with what it represented. On 6 October 1845 he walked out of the gates of his beloved seminary, crossed the street, entered a hotel room and changed into layman's clothing. This act was a symbolic and outward enactment of the steady conversion that had been stirring profoundly within his own life.[30] With undying gratitude to his former Catholic faith, Renan remained within it for some time after he left the priesthood. But eventually he came to believe that he had found a new faith that more fully satisfied him morally, emotionally, and intellectually. Like the Apostle Paul, who always found in his heart a deep respect for his Jewish heritage, Renan retained respect for his Catholic heritage even though his new religious commitments had replaced it.

Comparing Renan and Newman

The long religious journeys of Ernest Renan and John Henry Newman were *psychologically* very much alike. Each found it difficult to leave behind his old faith, partly because of friends and family ties. Fortunate indeed is the man or woman whose friends and family can extend their love over the walls of serious religious differences.

Renan and Newman were psychologically alike in other significant ways. Each started with the presumption of an error-free revelation and a God who provides such a revelation. Each started also with the

---

[29]Ernest Renan, *Recollections of My Youth*, trans. C. B. Pitman (London: George Routledge & Sons, 1929), p. 389.

[30]See Tsanoff, *Autobiographies*, pp. 186-87.

presupposition that this revelation had been deposited in an earthly book and an earthly Church. Newman moved away from Anglicanism into Roman Catholicism because he came to believe that it was the latter that God had chosen to be the guardian of his infallible revelation. Renan, who grew up and became a priest within the Roman Catholic Church, examined its credentials from the inside. In the long and painful process of carrying out the inquiry, this devout priest came to believe that neither the Bible nor his Church could stand firm as an unerring spokesman of God. He had not embarked on this inquiry alone, but was a member of the large community of devout Biblical scholars who were prepared to accept the challenge of proving and testing the faith. Out of his ordeal and test, Renan encountered a new faith awaiting him, but it was a faith that had grown out of the old one. His sense of history did not allow him to be bitter about his Roman Catholic background, for he recognized that French Catholicism had given him very much. But he did not turn his gratitude into slavish adoration or loss of courage to follow the new light and the new leads with zeal and commitment.

Renan's Life of Jesus

Like Albert Schweitzer who came after him, Ernest Renan was captured and inspired by the Jesus of the Gospels. To be sure, neither Renan nor Schweitzer was able to take the Gospels as an undistorted portrayal of Christ. Each scholar in his own way turned his Biblical training to the task of searching out the "real Jesus" behind the Gospels. Renan's remarkable book *Life of Jesus* has had a profound impact on many of those who would seek to understand more fully how Christianity was born in the Roman Empire.

In moving away from the dominating assumption of an infallible book and Church, Renan's own psychological structure underwent a transformation. The new vision of Jesus became for him a transforming vision that changed the direction of his life. While Renan remained in France for the rest of his life and continued to be a seeker of truth and a professed disciple of Jesus outside every formal Christian church, Schweitzer's studies of Jesus led him to write *The Quest for the Historical Jesus* and to enter medical school in order to prepare himself to become eventually a physician "on the edge of the primeval forest" in Africa.

The Conversion of Contemporary Roman Catholicism

It is one of the ironies of history that in our contemporary times Ernest Renan seems to many Catholics to be more Catholic than Cardinal Newman does. If Renan never ceased to express his debt of gratitude to his Catholic heritage, then perhaps contemporary Catholics will come to express a debt of gratitude to Ernest Renan. Pope John XXIII seemed to be more with Renan than Cardinal Newman when he reportedly said: "I'm infallible only when I speak ex cathedra. But I'll never speak ex cathedra." This quotation from the mouth of Pope John is recorded in the book *Infallible? An Inquiry,* which was written by the controversial theologian Hans Küng, who contends that infallibility is not a part of the essential Catholic faith.[31]

As for the doctrine of the infallibility of the Bible, a number of Roman Catholics and Protestant Biblical scholars regard the doctrine to be not only unnecessary but a hindrance to scholarly research. Indeed, the contemporary quest for the historical Jesus is among Roman Catholic students of the Bible something that Renan himself would doubtless applaud. The last two pages of Father Andrew M. Greeley's recent book on Jesus read as if they are deep reflections on Renan's *Life of Jesus.*[32]

It is important to understand that not only do individual lives undergo profound conversions, but entire religious movements, traditions, institutions and churches sometimes find themselves being transformed even "against their will." Buddhism represents a radical and lasting transformation that grew out of Hinduism. Christianity represents a transformation that grew out of the Hebrew faith as it encountered the Greek and Roman world of the first century. The Apostle Paul shared in this radical shift, and we will turn now to examine this most remarkable religious figure.

The Conversion of Paul: A Paradigm Case

Krister Stendahl holds that Paul did not go through a drastic religious conversion when he became a Christian. Despite our respect for Professor Stendahl's careful and esteemed scholarship, we take the more traditional position that Paul did experience a radical conversion and that Christianity is a radical shift from Judaism. In Chapter 6 we will examine the metaphysical content of this shift. In this chapter we will try to limit our inquiry to the psychological dimension of Paul's conversion. But before turning to that inquiry, we wish to note briefly that Paul justly stands as a paradigm of individuals who have experienced the new birth. He is in virtually every respect a twice-born person. To understand Paul

---

[31]Trans. Edward Quinn (Garden City, N.Y.: Doubleday, 1971), p. 87.

[32]See Andrew M. Greeley, *The Jesus Myth: New Insights into the Person and Message of Jesus* (Garden City, N.Y.: Image Books, Doubleday, 1973), pp. 197-98.

is to understand much about the structure of religious conversion or the second birth.

The Divided Self

In a deeply moving and revealing passage (Romans 7:14-25) the Apostle Paul tells of his own "inner" strife with himself. The passage is so frank, so disarmingly open, that some Christians have come to believe that the Apostle was writing not of himself as a Christian, but as he used to be *before* becoming a Christian. But, as the New Testament scholar C. H. Dodd points out, in leading into this famous passage, Paul dispenses with the past tense in order to take up the present tense. He does not say, "I *was* carnal, sold under sin," but rather "I am carnal, sold under sin" (Romans 7:14 RSV).

This self-confession on Paul's part is so vivid and insightful that we think it best to quote it directly before commenting on it:

> We know that the law is spiritual; but I am carnal, sold under sin. I do not understand my own actions. For I do not do what I want, but I do the very thing I hate. Now if I do what I do not want, I agree that the law is good. So then it is no longer I that do it, but sin which dwells within me. For I know that nothing good dwells within me, that is, in my flesh. I can will what is right, but I cannot do it. For I do not do the good I want, but the evil I do not want is what I do. Now if I do not do what I want, it is no longer I that do it, but sin which dwells within me.
>
> So I find it to be a law that when I want to do right, evil lies close at hand. For I delight in the law of God, in my inmost self, but I see in my members another law at war with the law of my mind and making me captive to the law of sin which dwells in my members. Wretched man that I am! Who will deliver me from this body of death? (Romans 7:14-24 RSV).

According to two evangelical Christian commentators, this passage has fundamentally to do with Paul's "inner conflict between what psychologists term the organized and disorganized self."[33] But this interpretation misses the force and power of Paul's war with himself. Paul sees his problem as stemming, not from a carnal self that is unorganized, but from one that is well organized. That is what he means by the *law* of sin in his members. "I see in my members another *law* of sin at war with the *law* of my mind and making me captive to the *law* of sin

---

[33]G. T. Thomson and F. Davidson, "The Epistle to the Romans," in F. Davidson, ed., *The New Bible Commentary*, 2nd ed. (Grand Rapids: Eerdmans, 1954), p. 952.

which dwells in my members" (italics added). Paul uses the term "law" in more than one way, but in this passage he seems to have in mind a very special order and structure that belongs to sin. Far from being a disorganized self, sin in the form of the carnal self is thought of by Paul as having its own organization, pattern, momentum, and direction. A wholly disorganized self is no self at all, and Paul sees himself as having a kind of subsidiary or satellite self that makes war on his more basic or "inmost" self. Sometimes the Apostle uses the pronoun 'I' to refer to either of these selves or to both of them together.

It is not altogether surprising, therefore, that this Apostle could write frankly, "I do not understand my own actions." It is not surprising because apparently he was not always entirely clear as to just who he was. Indeed, it is often true that one of the psychological motivations in the experience of conversion or being born again has to do with the problem of how to *identify oneself* in one's own mind. To be sure, a self-identity crisis stands in the background of every finite human being, but sometimes this crisis comes to the forefront to demand a resolution. To be born again is, psychologically speaking, a process of gaining a new identity, a new self.

A twentieth-century physicist, Wolfgang Pauli, suffered personally a self-identity crisis during the time that the field of physics was undergoing an unbelievably rapid and critical state of change. In the months before another famous physicist, Werner Heisenberg, gave his powerfully illuminating presentation on matrix mechanics, Professor Pauli wrote the following to a friend: "At the moment physics is again terribly confused. In any case, it is too difficult for me, and I wish I had been a movie comedian or something of the sort and had never heard of physics."[34] The meaningful work and values that the field of physics had provided him for many years were now under severe threat. As a result the physicist's own identity was threatened, for he had *identified* himself considerably with his work in physics and the values attached to it.

Fortunately, five months after writing this very pessimistic letter, he could write the following: "Heisenberg's type of mechanics has again given me hope and joy in life."[35] The crisis in physics itself produced an identity crisis in the life of one of its most noted servants, Wolfgang Pauli. Heisenberg's brilliant and revolutionary discoveries had helped

---

[34]Quoted in Thomas Kuhn, *The Structure of Scientific Revolutions*, 2nd ed. (Chicago: University of Chicago Press, 1970), p. 84.

[35]Ibid.

convert physics from a state of confusion to a meaningful system. As a consequence, Pauli's own life underwent a remarkable conversion. In his book *The Philosophical Impact of Contemporary Physics,* Professor Milič Čapek speaks of the physicist Louis de Broglie and "his conversion to indeterminism."[36] The word "conversion" here should not be skimmed over lightly, for the theoretical doctrines that men and women identify with can sometimes transform the very structure of their self-identity.

Conflicting Directions of the Self

A number of religious traditions divide the individual into two selves—the higher self and the lower self, or the inmost self and the outer self, or the true self and the false self, or the noble self and the perverse self. More accurately, each person may be thought of as *many* selves. In fact, there are still other ways to express the truth that the human individual is an incredibly complex creature who is sometimes in conflict with himself. We think it most fruitful to think of the individual as usually *one self* that ventures out in *multiple directions.* Each direction in which a self or person ventures is a system of behavior, which includes not only those overt behaviors observable to the public, but also private covert behaviors taking place inside the skin and head of the individual. This can be spelled out.

When a boy is practicing his piano lessons, he is engaging in certain private covert behaviors and certain public overt behaviors that are different from his behaviors when he is active on the baseball diamond. Doubtless, many a boy has suffered a measure of conflict and torment whenever these two systems of behavior—playing the piano and playing baseball—were in severe and direct conflict with one another. Psychologically, this is the same sort of conflict that a minister of a church might experience when he finds that he cannot at the same *time and place* prepare his sermons and attend the basketball tournament.

It would be misleading to tell the boy in conflict that his propensity to play baseball is by the nature of things the *lower* self, while his propensity to play the piano is the *higher* self. It is even more misleading to claim that one of these systems of behavior is the real or true self, while the other is the false or illusory self. The fact is that playing baseball or watching a basketball tournament is just as real as playing the piano or preparing sermons. Even though one system of behavior may be more

---

[36]Milič Čapek, *Philosophical Impact of Contemporary Physics* (Princeton, N.J.: D. Van Nostrand Co., 1961), p. 320.

desirable or praiseworthy than the other, each is as real as the other. However, very often when the members of a church or community choose not to recognize a certain activity or style of behavior as *legitimate,* they fall into the habit of thinking that the activity is somehow not a *reality.* Mary Baker Eddy carried this practice to the extreme when she wrote into Christian Science teaching the doctrine that all evil is really error. Later, we will speak more fully of both "the social construction of reality" and "the social destruction of reality."

The Tragedy of Divided Loyalties

When the convert begins to suffer divided loyalties—one loyalty to the church and another to the family or to another community—the issue usually becomes one of either conflicting values or conflicting schedules. The conflict of schedule is comparatively much easier to resolve than the entangled conflict of values. When the conflict is indeed one of the fundamental values, then the convert may find himself in the position of the child who must choose which one of his divorcing parents he will live with.

In some cases, the religious conversion resolves conflicts for the individual only to inflict on him even more serious conflicts. For centuries, Biblical scholars have, understandably, been perplexed by the following quotation attributed to Jesus:

> I came to cast fire upon the earth; and would that it were already kindled! I have a baptism to be baptized with; and how I am constrained until it is accomplished! Do you think that I have come to give peace on earth? No, I tell you, but rather division; for henceforth in one house there will be five divided, three against two and two against three; they will be divided, father against son and son against father, mother against daughter and daughter against mother, mother-in-law against her daughter-in-law and daughter-in-law against her mother-in-law (Luke 12:49-53 RSV).

Our conclusion is that for human relationships, religious conversion always has its tragic side. The Prince of Peace brings fire as well as peace. It is a notorious fact that in the attempt to bring oneness and unity among mankind, religious movements have created dissension and even strife. Othodox Marxists promise that the classless society will surely and inevitably come—but only with force and violence. The ultimate and perfect harmony that most religions promise seems to elude them all. Even in the vision of the next life, the orthodox Muslims and Christians portray a scene in which violence is perpetrated without end on unbelievers in hell.

Whether the vision of perfect harmony creates in the "psyche" more overall frustration and disappointment than the "psyche" would have experienced without the vision is not an easy question to answer. Nevertheless, it is safe to say that when considered from a purely psychological perspective, millions of people appear to have found religious conversion to be a doorway to something much better than what had been their lot in life before their conversion. But where this has not turned out to be the case, some converts have moved further on in quest of still another faith that promises to bind up their wounded hearts and to give them some security against the sea of chaos that threatens all finite human existence.

The Psychology of the Desperate Creature

It is not surprising that the human creature would seek to be born again, that is, born into a realm where somehow death and meaninglessness do not have the final word. As the existentialists have noted in so many ways, the human creature is a being-unto-death, and it is still open to question as to whether the majority of mankind could psychologically cope successfully if they should come to believe that there is in fact no life after death. Some students of religion contend that religion offers the only way for the most desperate of all earthly creatures to handle the fact of his earthly demise. However, other students of religion contend that most religions serve to rob human beings of the opportunity of facing death realistically, courageously, and with minimum illusion.

One noted psychologist of religion states this second position candidly:

> Psychoanalytic investigators, noting how often religious belief
> is buttressed by speculations about individual immortality, and
> vice versa, have correctly pointed to a persistent core of
> grandiosity in some religious formulations of "life after
> death." Empirically, some people are humble enough not to
> demand immortality for themselves, and they may regard
> themselves irreligious; others, more likely to call themselves
> religious, humiliate themselves now before their gods in order
> to assure their eventual continuity after death.[37]

But there are still other students of the psychological dimension of religious conversion who contend that few people are emotionally and

---

[37]Paul W. Pruyser, "Problems of Definition and Conception in the Psychological Study of Unbelief," in Allan W. Eister, ed., *Changing Perspectives in the Scientific Study of Religion* (New York: John Wiley and Sons, 1974), p. 189.

intellectually equipped to find meaning in living if they come to believe that they will never finally overcome the ultimate enemy—death. Accordingly, it is judged to be more humane to leave the majority of humanity with their "illusion of immortality" than to leave them exposed defenseless before the thought of their absolute and final extinction. Needless to say, the question still remains: Is there really life after death? *No answer to this question can be found by making psychological inquiries only.* How it can be answered is itself a matter of debate.

Summary

In this chapter we have tried to locate the taproot of the psychological dimension of religious conversion. We concluded that the taproot is the individual's sense of his own finiteness and absolute dependency. While individuals may be mistaken either about what in particular they depend upon or the manner of their dependency, they nevertheless are reminded in countless ways that they are not self-maintained entities in the world.

Facing their finitude, individuals respond largely against the background of their cultural environment. Their culture sets the stage for the way that they formulate and come to terms with their sense of absolute dependency. Renan, Newman, and Wesley are examples of those who inherited from their culture and from their historical context an expectation that an infallible authority would give them assurance against the threat of finitude, chaos and confusion.

Because each human being is finite, he *must* begin his life with expectations that he did not "choose." They are as much a part of his constitution as are his bones and blood. What happens to those expectations during his life is to some extent the story of each "pilgrim's progress."

Finally, we have tried to stress the point that the psychological dimension of religion takes on meaning only when the inquiry moves beyond the individual's personal feelings and responses in order to see them in the larger social and cultural context of inherited belief-systems, personal associations, and other connections with the world beyond the believer's private "inner" experience.[38] We now turn to look more carefully into what may be called the *structure and setting* of the new birth process.

---

[38]Those interested in the controversy as to whether private experiences have causal power may wish to consult Roger Schnaitler, "Private Causes," *Behaviorism: A Forum for Critical Discussion*, 6:1 (Spring, 1978), 1-12.

Chapter III

The Role of Vision and Voices in the New Birth

Two Styles of Conversion

In his book *The Varieties of Religious Experience,* the noted American psychologist and philosopher William James distinguishes the once-born believer from the twice-born. We have been considerably influenced by this remarkable book, but our position is that every socialized individual has been twice-born.[1] This may sound strange to a number of readers until we explain that we are making only a psychological and sociological judgment at this point. Whether this twice-born process is also a supernatural phenomenon in *all* cases, in *some* cases only, or in *none* of them is a question that we will delve into in a later chapter.

We think it more fruitful at the psychological level to distinguish (1) the second birth that comes gradually from (2) the second birth that comes with trauma and travail. It is probably an error to suggest that one of these is more natural than the other, or that one is more authentic than the other. Each style of conversion or new birth has its special advantages and disadvantages.

---

[1]See William James, *The Varieties of Religious Experience: A Study in Human Nature* (New York: Modern Library, 1902), Lecture 8.

The Traumatic Conversion

Because the traumatic conversion is more dramatic, it is likely to be more exciting to read about. One characteristic of the turbulent new birth is that it faces with greater intensity and anxiety the fact of human finitude. Indeed, in cases of the traumatic conversion, the individual has ordinarily suffered a kind of *shock* in being confronted with some dimension of his own utter helplessness. Because of this shock and critical disturbance of mind, he is unable to move smoothly into a new birth. The transition from this state of shock does not move smoothly for the simple reason that the sense of helplessness seems to have an unyielding grip on him. Preoccupied with the awareness of his utter finitude, he seems unable to deal with life without this topic somehow swamping his thoughts, feelings, and actions.

In many cases, this critical state of mind cannot be dealt with apart from some very powerful and equally dramatic breakthrough. It is in such cases that some form of vision may enter the scene to serve as a powerful and dramatic influence. The vision serves literally to move the individual out of his crisis and into a state where he can overcome some of the effects of the shock-of-finitude that he has suffered. This is not to say that some powerful vision is always required in the severe religious crisis which we will call *finitude shock*. A businessman in Tennessee once revealed that when he was twenty-one years old he went through an entire year of preoccupation with the realization that someday he would die. It was a tormenting experience of finitude shock which eventually subsided in the way that a fever sometimes seems to subside with no conspicuously dramatic cause. But in the same city in Tennessee a few years later, a woman (whom we will call Barbara Nelson) in her early thirties was experiencing the sense of utter helplessness when a powerful vision entered her life and transformed it.

The Appearance of the Deceased Husband

Barbara Nelson's husband, Mark, had recently suffered a heart attack and was in the hospital. As a nurse, Barbara knew the seriousness of her husband's condition and had remained at the hospital for well over a week until the crisis seemed to pass. Mark's doctor assured her that she was not needed at the hospital and could go home to rest. Immediately upon arriving at the house, Barbara heard the phone ring and answered it. The news was devastating. Mark had just died.

As Barbara related this story to us, she proceeded to explain that after this initial shock eventually subsided somewhat, she was flooded with incurable feelings of guilt. She began going to the graveside of her husband to pray, asking God to let her talk to Mark just once. She longed for some word of comfort and reassurance from her husband, some communication from the man who had been a gentle and kind human being. But as her prayers remained unanswered, her anxiety intensified.

Perpetually confused and able to gain only minimum orientation in her life, Barbara lacked both direction and confidence, and seemed not to know what to do about the endless list of responsibilities that had fallen on her and her four children. "I was out of my mind," she kept saying to us.

Finally, one day this nurse went to the bathroom and poured into her hand a large number of pills. But before getting them into her mouth, she heard one of her children cry in the backyard. Without hesitation, she rushed out to rescue her child. To make the story short, the child was rescued, but during this episode a strong and remarkable phenomenon took place. Her husband Mark appeared visibly and audibly to her and told her that he was doing well and that she would someday come to be with him. Mark went on to encourage Barbara to take care of the children and to pursue her nursing career.

Believing that she had in fact talked with her husband, Barbara found this powerful and dramatic experience to be the needed turning point in her life. Suicide no longer seemed a genuine option to her; her life began to take on a new commitment and definite direction. In addition, her intense anxiety disappeared. In short, the experience of seeing and conversing with her deceased husband had effected a profound and lasting transformation in her life. She was converted from aimless and ineffective wandering to a bold woman setting out on a remarkable career with a set of clear goals. Today, she has her own business and is doing an outstanding work in influencing her state legislature to pass laws to protect and assist the aged. The transformation in the woman's life was and is astounding.

Our concern here is not to delve into the question of whether Mark was really and objectively standing in the presence of Barbara on that pivotal day when she almost committed suicide. When in the course of our conversation she pressed us and insisted that we agree with her that Mark was "really" there, we replied in the following way. First, we noted that as a nurse she was doubtless familiar with the fact that sometimes a person who has had an arm amputated will thereafter still feel the fingers even though they are not objectively there. Second, we offered the theory that the appearance of her husband Mark was something of a vision rather than an objectively real presence. In other words, it was real as a *subjective* experience; but by *taking* it to be objectively real at the time,

Barbara was enabled to be deeply moved and affected by the experience. The *consequence of believing* the vision to be real was certainly real, for the transformation in her life can hardly be denied.

Our conjecture is that given her frame of reference and her strong expectations, Barbara's finitude shock needed something dramatic and powerful to bring her out of her state of helplessness and acute depression. It was as if the vision of Mark was a very potent medicine required to overcome the severe effects that her husband's death and her own guilt had produced.

Visions and voices have played a significant role in the lives of individuals and societies of every generation and on every continent of the earth. Psychologists and philosophers disagree among themselves as to whether visions and voices have any *causal influence* on the individual's behavior, since they are private experiences only. The position known as radical behaviorism denies that the visions and voices are causes at all. Rather they are regarded as *effects* of external causes and conditions. We will not in this book follow that debate, but rather say simply that we differ with radical behaviorism on this one point. We hold that visions and voices, even though they are private and subjective, nevertheless may have an *impact*—a profound impact—on the individual experiencing them.*

The Vision of the Apostle Peter

The lives of some of the early Christians were profoundly and lastingly shaped by visions. The Apostle Peter had an experience that significantly influenced his life. According to the Book of Acts, he

> saw the heaven opened, and something descending, like a great sheet, let down by four corners upon the earth. In it were all kinds of animals and reptiles and birds of the air. And there came a voice to him, "Rise, Peter, kill and eat." But Peter said, "No Lord; for I have never eaten anything that is common or unclean." And the voice came to him again the second time, "What God has cleansed you must not call common." This happened three times, and the thing was taken up at once to heaven (Acts 10:11-16 RSV).

Just as Barbara Nelson was seeking some communication from her husband, so Peter seems to have been searching for some communication from his Lord regarding what attitude he should take toward Christian

---

*See footnote 38 of chapter 2.

Gentiles. After all, even though Christians, they still ate what he as a Jew regarded as common or unclean food. We know from the second chapter of Paul's letter to the Galatians that Peter was very ambivalent about his relationships with Gentile Christians. Paul reported that Peter actually ate at the same table with Gentiles until some of the representatives of "the circumcision party" of James exerted pressure on him. Yielding to this pressure, Peter "drew back and separated himself" from eating with the Gentile Christians. Paul rebuked Peter to his face for doing this and even accused him of acting insincerely. A more charitable explanation would have been that Peter was acting inconsistently and ambivalently. In any case, Peter was certainly being pressured by Paul from one direction and by the representatives of James from the other direction. So, it should be no surprise to learn that he was desperate for special communication from his Lord on the matter.

Peter's experience of hearing the voice and seeing the great sheet descending from heaven is classified in the Book of Acts as a "vision." Before relating the content of Peter's vision, the author of the Book of Acts stated that Peter first "fell into a trance." The author nevertheless made it clear that this vision had a powerful influence on Peter's subsequent thinking and behavior regarding Gentiles.

The Appearances of Christ

In I Corinthians 15 the Apostle Paul contended that the resurrected Christ appeared to Peter, to the twelve, to more than five hundred brethren at one time, to James, to all the apostles, and last of all to Paul himself. It is interesting that Paul made no distinction between his own personal experience of the resurrected Christ and the experiences of these other men. (He made no reference to Christ's appearance to women.)

If we rely on the Book of Acts for the account of Paul's conversion experience, it would seem that the appearances of Christ mentioned in I Corinthians 15 were quite similar in nature to Peter's vision or Mark Nelson's appearance to his wife Barbara. That is, they were more *subjective* than *objective* in nature. This needs further clarification.

According to the two accounts given in the Book of Acts (9:3-8; 22:6-11), neither Paul nor his traveling companions *saw* Christ, not even in a vision. Rather, Paul heard a voice, even though the companions apparently did not. According to the second account (22:6-11), the companions did see a bright light at this noon hour in the desert. Of course, they could hardly help observing Paul's very strange behavior and doubtless concluded that something unusual was surely going on.

The point here is that Paul had no clearly *objective* experience as we use the word today, and there is no strong reason to conclude that he thought that the other men—over five hundred of them—had what we would today regard as an experience of something objectively real. It is quite interesting that Paul made no mention either of any women who experienced the resurrected Christ or of an empty tomb. Indeed, theologian Emil Brunner takes a position which many other Christian Biblical scholars today take, namely, that the "resurrection appearances" of Christ were not publicly observable events. Other people could not have "seen" or "heard" this Christ by simply being in the vicinity at a particular time. Or, stated in another way, if cameras had been invented in the first century, the "appearances" of the resurrected Jesus could not have been captured on film. Brunner seems to believe that a person wandering by at the time when Christ was preaching before his death would have been able to see and hear him. Christ's presence was publicly observable at that time. But after his death, Christ was never publicly observable.[2]

Various attempts have been made to organize in a coherent picture Paul's account of the appearances of Christ with the appearances mentioned in the Gospels, but no such coherent picture has come about.[3] In more recent years, even the evangelical Christian Biblical scholar Dewey Beegle has concluded that the Biblical passages dealing with the resurrection of Christ "swarm with difficulties, some details of which cannot be harmonized."[4]

But our primary purpose here is not to review the pros and cons of the theory of the physical appearances of Christ after his death, but rather to emphasize the important role of vision in the conversion or new birth process. There is no doubt that even if the appearances of Christ were not objective, they nevertheless were very powerful influences on the lives of some of the early Christians, just as Barbara Nelson's experience of Mark powerfully influenced her life. This is not to say that every Christian has had an experience comparable to that of the early apostles, although many today who speak of being born again claim to have some "experience of the living Christ" in their lives. Later, we will look into this claim.

---

[2]See Emil Brunner, *The Christian Doctrine of Creation and Redemption; Dogmatics:* Vol. II, trans. Olive Wyon (London: Lutterworth Press, 1952), p. 328.

[3]See ibid., pp. 366-68.

[4]Dewey Beegle, *Scripture, Tradition, and Infallibility* (Grand Rapids: Eerdmans, 1973), p. 61.

Reflection on Visions

Even though she was a member of a Protestant Church, Barbara Nelson was not knowledgeable in the technical details of Protestant theology. Had she been, she very likely would not have prayed either to see Mark or to talk with him, for talking with the dead is not regarded as in line with traditional Protestant theological belief.

Jody Row (as we will call her) lost her husband after forty-five years of marriage. As a Southern Baptist and a woman well-versed in the Bible and knowledgeable in Protestant theology, she never prayed to see her husband after his death. Nevertheless, she related the following to one of us. At various times after his death she would hear him come in the back door, close it and exclaim in his exuberant voice, "Honey, I'm home!" That is what he almost always said when he returned from work or a trip. Jody Row had never told her grown children of this because she was embarrassed about it. She did not believe that her husband was actually entering the house as he had always done, but she was embarrassed because she could not help having the experience now and then. One of us explained that such an experience was not uncommon for widows or widowers and that it was, in fact, quite normal. She was advised: "Go ahead and have the experience, and let it remind you of the good times that the two of you had together over the years. This may be one of the memories that you will want to cherish for many years."

Many people have visions and hear voices, but how they are *interpreted* depends largely on the theological or metaphysical background of the person. Jody Row confessed that she had been and still was terribly lonely. Again, she had not confided this to her children. "They have their lives to live," she remarked. Nevertheless, it was clear that the voice that she heard—"Honey, I'm home!"—was a great comfort to her even though she took it to be subjective rather than objective. She regarded it as more of a memory than an actual voice of an objective person literally entering the door. She related all this to one of us because she needed to have a close friend to agree with her that (1) she was quite sane and (2) she was not simply self-indulgent because she had allowed herself to have the experience and to receive considerable comfort from it.

Even though she took the voice to be subjective, it was still quite influential in helping her to cope with her state of loneliness, which in her case created an unmistakable sense of finitude. More than she had realized, she was still *absolutely dependent* on *human* relationships for her well-being. She was more dependent and more vulnerable than she had realized. Our point here is that if this experience was quite important to her coping successfully with her finitude, how much more influential might it have been (for good or ill) had she taken the voice to be, not a subjective experience only, but the voice of an objective spirit in her kitchen! We will argue later that for centuries the lives of most people were partially controlled and guided by voices they heard and visions they saw.

Functional Dreams

It is sometimes forgotten that both science and religion are a rich part of human culture and that without dreams and visions, both science and religion would have perished from human life. It is also forgotten at times that some of the great scientific and philosophical visions were taken by their agents as transforming religious experiences. Many scientists have committed themselves to the search for Truth in the way that other people have dedicated their lives to the search for God. But like God, Truth may reveal itself through visions and dreams. No one can see Pure Truth and live. Visions and mighty dreams both reveal and conceal.

It may sound strange to some people to hear that dreams and visions often play a profound role in the growth of scientific knowledge. But the nineteenth century chemist F. A. Kekule remarked, "Let us learn to dream, gentlemen, then perhaps we shall find the truth."[5] Creative scientists and philosophers have always learned to dream.

We think the following passage from a philosopher of science is worth quoting because it reminds us of some aspects of the traumatic religious conversion:

> A noteworthy characteristic of flashes of insight, if we are to accept the reports of scientists who have had them, is that they almost always produce in the minds of their originators an overwhelming conviction of truth. Not only does the idea itself appear suddenly, but the whole set of the mind is instantly changed from one of puzzlement, perplexity, and tension, to one characterized by that peace of mind which is found only when problems have been solved and difficulties overcome.[6]

We recall Professor Wolfgang Pauli's experience of renewed "hope and joy in life" when a new and creative metaphysical scheme was

---

[5]Quoted from Bernard Barber, *Science and the Social Order* (Chicago: The Free Press of Glencoe, 1952), p. 203.

[6]Benjamin Cornelius, *Science, Technology, and Human Values* (Columbia: University of Missouri Press, 1965), pp. 111-12.

introduced into the confused field of physics in his lifetime. We recall also that "peace of mind" was claimed by Paul, Buddha, Ernest Renan, John Henry Newman, John Wesley, and many others who experienced a profound religious conversion.

Hearing and Obeying the Voices

There is no guarantee that dreams or visions will plug into reality. They may turn out to be quite insane or at least fantasies without substance. If they are to provide insight, they need to be tested, criticized, compared with rival dreams and visions, and formulated in a variety of ways to make them yield fruit, that is, to make them enriching to the growth of knowledge.

Understandably, people sometimes resist having their visions subjected to rational debate, critical scrutiny, or compared with other visions. There was once a time in the history of mankind when visions, dreams, and especially voices were simply obeyed with little or no hesitation of mind. As late as the famous *Iliad* of the Greeks—sometime between 1250 and 850 B.C.—individuals did not think in a conscious way as we do today. We hold that the intense notion of self-consciousness and ego that we take for granted in our culture did not develop for hundreds of thousands of years after the human species originated. Men and women acted in response to cues and in response especially to voices they heard. The current vogue in psychiatry tends to label as "schizophrenic"* those who hear voices and take these voices so seriously as to obey their commands. But in the time of the bards of the *Iliad*, and centuries before that, the voices were a normal part of life. Even in our ordinary speech today we still carry some of the residue of that ancient time when we speak of the "voice of conscience" or the "voice of reason," although in most cases we hear no literal voices telling us what to do.

The Bicameral Mind

We are in considerable agreement with Julian Jaynes' book, *The Origin of Consciousness in the Breakdown of the Bicameral Mind,* in which he advances the brilliant and daring hypothesis that "at one time human nature was split in two, an executive part called a god, and a follower part called a man. Neither part was conscious."[7] There is little doubt that even

---

*The entire notion of "schizophrenia" has recently come under severe attack by psychologists Theodore R. Sarbin and James C. Mancuso in *Schizophrenia: Medical Diagnosis or Moral Verdict?* (New York: Pergamon Press, 1980) and by psychiatrist Thomas S. Szasz in *Schizophrenia: Sacred Symbol of Psychiatry* (New York: Basic Books, 1976).

[7](Boston: Houghton Mifflin Co., 1977), chapter 3.

today a considerable amount of important thinking is done more or less unconsciously. When driving a car, brushing our teeth, typing, peeling a banana, and engaging in a thousand and one other such activities, we are not always fully conscious. Nevertheless we are thinking. Indeed, some thinking is done more efficiently if it is done with less consciousness—for example, in typing.

Professor Jaynes' theory of the bicameral mind is too involved to spell out in this book; nevertheless we do wish to point out that according to this theory, the right side of the human brain (for right-handed people) was to take in the cues and stimuli of its environment, decode the stimuli, and then transmit the resultant "message" to the rest of the body, thus moving it into action. But, Professor Jaynes contends, there were situations when the process was not so smooth. In order to transform the incoming stimuli into overt bodily behavior and actions, something additional was required. It was external command! But the rulers, fathers, and other authority figures could not always be present to issue the external commands. Hence, the individual learned to produce *unconsciously* a commanding voice *from inside his own brain.* But he did not realize that the source of the voice was his own brain. To him, it was an external, authoritative, commanding voice, which he tended to identify with his father, ruler, or authority figure.

Even today, some people have this sort of experience in rare periods of crisis, although not all of these people regard the "voice" to be the word or voice of God. Professor Jaynes relates the following experience which he had:

> One afternoon I lay down in intellectual despair on a couch. Suddenly, out of an absolute quiet, there came a firm, distinct loud voice from my upper right which said, "Include the knower in the known!" It lugged me to my feet absurdly exclaiming, "Hello?" looking for whoever was in the room. The voice had an exact location. No one was there! Not even behind the wall where I sheepishly looked. I do not take this nebulous profundity as divinely inspired, but I do think it is similar to what was heard by those who have in the past claimed such special selection.[8]

Professor Jaynes goes on to say that after giving his lecture on his theory of the bicameral mind, he is often surprised at the number of people in the audience who come up afterward to tell of voices they had heard. He goes on to say that for some people today, these voices may be

---

[8]Ibid., p. 86.

accompanied by visual hallucinations.[9]

A man named Larry Jayson was with some companions on a sunny day at Coney Island when suddenly he rose to his feet and walked into the Atlantic Ocean to drown himself. Fortunately, he was rescued by lifeguards. What caused this man to attempt suicide? Later, through the help and acceptance of therapists, he felt free to explain that he was obeying a deep voice, which was so loud and clear that he assumed that everyone around him had also heard it. The voice stated in authoritative tones that Larry Jayson was "no good."

> "You're no good," the voice said slowly, in the same deep tones. "You've never been any good or use on earth. There is the ocean. You might just as well drown yourself. Just walk in, and keep walking." As soon as the voice was through, I knew by its cold command I had to obey it.[10]

The noted American evangelist and college president, Jonathan Edwards, told of the following that took place in one of his revival meetings in New England. People claimed to see "the piercing all-seeing eye of God"; on one occasion a man was driven to suicide by cutting his own throat. The multitude, strangely moved by this example, *heard voices* urging them, "Cut your own throat, now is a good opportunity." Edwards wrote that the people "were obliged to fight with all their might to resist it."[11]

Fortunately, not all voices have commanded such self-destructive acts. Amos the prophet heard a voice which commanded him to defend the claims of the poor, who had been shamelessly exploited by the rich. Many people have heard voices which they took to be commands of God to do good to others. Moses heard a voice located in a burning bush, a voice commanding him to be a liberator of a slave people. Jonathan Edwards wrote that some of the people in the New England revivals not only heard voices, but, like Moses, saw flames.[12] The Bible is filled with statements that the word (or voice) of the Lord came to various prophets.

The Decline of the Voices

As the voices began to be heard less frequently, people had to turn to the very few people who still heard the "voice of God." Jeremiah was one

---

[9]See ibid., p. 87.

[10]L. N. Jayson, *Mania* (New York: Funk and Wagnall, 1937), pp. 1-3.

[11]Jonathan Edwards, *Narrative of Many Surprising Conversions in Northampton and Vicinity: Together with Some Thoughts on the Revival of Religion in New England* (Worcester, Mass., 1832), pp. 74-75, 134-35.

[12]See ibid., p. 134.

such specialist in hearing the voice of God and passing the divine judgment on to others (see Jeremiah 42). The prophet sometimes was angry that the voice was not heeded. For him, it simply had to be obeyed:

> For you sent me to the Lord your God saying, "Pray for us to
> the Lord our God, and whatever the Lord our God says declare
> to us and we will do it." And I have this day declared it to you,
> but you have not obeyed the voice of the Lord your God in
> anything that he sent me to tell you (Jeremiah 42:20-21 RSV).

Jeremiah's preaching dates about 600 B.C., which is many centuries after the bicameral mind had begun to break down. In Jeremiah's time, people still had some fear of the voice; but when they went home or to the fields after hearing the prophet's report of the voice, the message lost some of its force. In earlier times, people out in the fields or at home would hear voices directly for themselves. But in Jeremiah's century, the voices were heard mostly by prophets and priests, rarely by the average man or woman.

The Return of the Golden Age

In every century there were those who longed for the time when once again the voice of God would be heard directly by each individual. Jeremiah predicted that the day would come when people will not have to learn about God from their neighbors but will know him directly: "for they shall all know me, from the least of them to the greatest, says the Lord" (Jeremiah 1:34 RSV).

On the famous day of Pentecost, Peter referred to the Biblical passage which promises that someday God will pour out his Spirit upon *everyone*:

> And in the last days it shall be, God declares,
> that I will pour out my Spirit upon all flesh,
> and your sons and your daughters shall prophesy,
> and your young men shall see visions,
> and your old men shall dream dreams;
> yea, and on my menservants and my maidservants in those
> days
> I will pour out my Spirit; and they shall prophesy
> (Acts 2:17-18 RSV; citing Joel 2:28-29).

The vague memory of how it used to be in times past had been preserved and passed on from generation to generation. Indeed, the early Christians seem to believe that they were coming into the last days, when God would reveal himself directly without the priesthood. Paul wrote, "The gospel which was preached by me is not man's gospel" (Galatians

1:11 RSV). Which is to say, it is not a second-hand report. Paul went on to say, "For I did not receive it from man, nor was I taught it, but it came through a revelation of Jesus Christ" (Galatians 1:11-12 RSV). Even the author of I Clement (chapter 63) claims he wrote his letter to Corinth through direct revelation from the Spirit. According to Mark 13:11, when Christians are arrested and brought to court, they do not need to prepare a case because the Holy Spirit will tell them directly what to say. The New Testament scholar J. Jeremias contends that early Christian prophets "addressed congregations in words of encouragement, admonition, censure and promise, using the name of Christ in the *first person*."[13]

The Confusion of Voices

In a complex, diverse and pluralistic society, confusion will likely increase when everyone thinks he hears and repeats the voice of the deity or saviour directly. To many mainline Christians today, the charismatics seem to symbolize this threat of confusion. In *The Origin of Consciousness in the Breakdown of the Bicameral Mind*, Professor Jaynes, we recall, contends that many centuries ago virtually everyone was commanded by voices. But those were simpler times, before the large-scale intermingling of different societies with their diverse and strange cultures. Great upheaval and a series of physical eruptions in the Aegean area set off a huge procession of mass migrations and invasions which wrecked the Hittite and Mycenaean empires. Without warning, whole populations or what survived of them were suddenly found to be wandering, confused refugees, like hungry dogs, invading their neighbors, and being in turn hunted down by neighbors. In such a tragic time, approximating chaos, what could the simple, tradition-oriented voices and gods command the helpless individuals to do?

The collapse under the ocean of a good part of the Aegean people's land, followed by a series of mass eruptions of the volcano on the islands of Therra, barely sixty-two miles north of Crete—such catastrophes in the physical environment sometime around 1180 B.C. could not do otherwise than create catastrophes in the lives of the peoples of the entire Mediterranean world. Cyprus, the Nile delta, and the coast of Israel suffered unspeakable calamity of a magnitude hardly believable.[14]

Travel, writing, and a modest degree of migration had already begun to affect the bicameral outlook, with its simple voices. But the shocking

---

[13]J. Jeremias, *New Testament Theology*, Part 1: *The Proclamation of Jesus*, trans. J. Bowdens (New York: Scribners, 1971), p. 2. Italics added.

[14]See Jaynes, *The Origin of Consciousness*, pp. 212-17.

physical eruptions especially in the twelfth century B.C. served to accelerate the breakdown of the bicameral way of life. Suddenly ordinary people were thrown into contact with other ordinary people who were guided by "the voice." But "the voices"—"the gods"—were not the same, since they were each coming out of a different culture. The conflict of voices and gods could not help but create conflict and confusion in the individual. Indeed, this conflict of cultures had already begun to develop on a more modest scale long before the great physical eruptions, and the sense of conflict and confusion sometimes was powerful and intense even if it was not widespread.

A striking example of this may be found in the case of Abraham, whose God tells him that his son Isaac will bear him grandchildren who, in turn, will benefit the nations. Later, however, when Isaac is born and becomes an active boy, a commanding voice tells Abraham to kill Isaac, his first and only son. This sort of conflict of authoritative voices was indeed enough to make Abraham somewhat conscious and hesitant, and it is not surprising that the Bible speaks of Abraham's arguing with the divine voice on one occasion. Apparently, Abraham had received two messages—one that God is just, the other that this God requires Abraham to go along with Him in supporting an unjust act (see Genesis 18:22-27). It is as if Abraham, like the perplexed father in *Fiddler on the Roof*, is saying, "On the one hand . . . , but on the other hand . . ."[15] It is the bicameral brain, the two sides, beginning to challenge and question one another.

Controlling the Voices

In one of his letters to the church at Corinth, the Apostle Paul had to deal with the problem of too many, rather than too few, prophetic voices in the church. A prophet in the early Christian movement was regarded as someone with the gift of receiving revelations directly from heaven or the realm of the spirit. But confusion at best, chaos at worst, seemed to threaten the Corinthian church when numerous prophets began releasing their revelations before the congregation. In order to control the rising epidemic of revelations, Paul insisted that the prophets speak one by one, each waiting his turn, and each listening to the other.

This procedure alone, ordinary as it seems to us today, was actually Paul's strategy for subjecting the prophetic utterances to social and institutional control. Imagine telling a prophet, in his moment of ecstasy

---

[15]Joseph Stein, *Fiddler on the Roof* (New York: Pocket Books, 1966), pp. 50, 73, 124, 148.

and intense inspiration, that he must in effect force "the spirit of prophets" to wait, hold back, until the human social institution was ready to receive the revelation. If in those days the prophet was seen as a kind of medium through which the spirit spoke directly and in first-person singular, then Paul's charge that the prophets delay their speaking was *in effect* a technique for leading them to *reflect* on their revelations. A prophet who must reflect on revelation is a prophet who may be forced to *revise or modify* his revelation, especially when he must listen to the utterances of other prophets. Paul's seemingly modest charge was in reality a major step toward what the sociologist Max Weber described as the *rationalization process,* which is not to be confused with the psychiatric notion of a defense mechanism.

Prophecy and the Rationalization Process

What does it mean to subject the prophetic revelations to the rationalization process? It means that the revelations will no longer be taken entirely at face value. The several revelations must be checked one against the other. And in the process of doing this, each revelation will itself undergo a certain refinement or clarification. For example, a revelation will be forced to specify more precisely and exactly its meaning and, in turn, be made to compete with other prophetic revelations through what in effect becomes a *comparative analysis.*

A modern example of the rationalization process may be found in a major decision of the directions of the *700 Club,* which is a popular charismatic program on what is billed as a Christian television network. The directors met to discuss whether or not there would be "speaking in tongues" on the television program. Even though the directors themselves believed strongly in speaking in tongues and regarded it as a powerful manifestation of the Spirit, they nevertheless made the decision that speaking in tongues would not be permitted on the televised *700 Club.* What this decision means in effect is this: the Holy Spirit may indeed move a born-again charismatic Christian to speak in tongues, but *not* on the televised *700 Club!* Paul himself had been forced to initiate in the first century a social mechanism for controlling speaking in tongues in public. Like the directors of the *700 Club,* he grew very concerned about the negative public relations impact that speaking in tongues might create (see I Corinthians 14:23, 27).

The rationalization process is seen in a curious passage (I Corinthians 14:32) in which Paul told the prophets themselves to control "the spirit of prophets." This passage is subject to more than one interpretation, but we suggest the following: Among the early Christians (as well as among other religious groups of the first century), many people believed that certain *contact persons* were in direct communication with the *spirit of prophets.* This spirit was vaguely thought of as either God or a heavenly messenger of God or even a gradation of God.

When the spirit of prophets came upon the contact individual, the latter fell more or less under the control of the spirit. That is, the contact person or prophet heard the revelation and spoke it directly. The Apostle Paul, however, seemed to insist on reforming this process by charging the prophets themselves to exert control over the spirit of prophets.

Looking at this strange passage from a naturalistic perspective, we are prone to think that the prophets in Paul's time were hallucinating the voices, that is, hearing voices from their own heads rather than hearing objective voices outside them. The sociocultural climate of the first century, however, had created a framework for *interpreting* the voices as being *supernatural* in both origin and content. Paul's charge that the prophets gain control over the spirit (i.e., voice) is, therefore, exceedingly suggestive for our understanding of contemporary religious conversions.

We recall that Paul had heard what he interpreted to be the voice of a cosmic being to whom he gave the titles or names Christ, Lord, Jesus, and Savior. Earlier in this chapter we pointed out that sometimes when they have powerful flashes of insight, scientists experience an overwhelming conviction of the truth of the insight. They cannot easily doubt its truth. Similarly, Paul received what he believed to be the insight or revelation to exceed all others. And he could not think of doubting it.

Paul regarded himself as an *apostle*, which was a stage higher than a prophet. Apostles are first. Prophets are second (I Corinthians 12:28). When translated into church politics, this means that Paul the apostle could challenge the revelation of a prophet, although a prophet could not challenge an apostle's revelation. To be sure, there were those at the time who regarded themselves to be apostles but whose "revelations" were at odds with Paul's. But since he was unable to doubt his own revelations, he did not hesitate to regard rival apostles as "false apostles."

All this has a modern ring to it. Today, we may observe preachers and charismatic leaders freely denounce one another as "false prophets" or even as agents of Satan. Even though we do not know altogether what was taking place behind the scenes in the Corinthian church, we do know that Paul was very angry with some who regarded themselves as apostles possessing "revelations" apparently different from his own. In very irate language he wrote:

> For such men are false apostles, deceitful workmen, disguising themselves as apostles of Christ. And no wonder, for even Satan

disguises himself as an angel of light. So it is not strange if his servants also disguise themselves as servants of righteousness (II Corinthians 11:13-15 RSV).

It was psychologically impossible for Paul to believe that an individual could sincerely regard himself as an apostle if that individual's "revelation" stood significantly in disagreement with Paul's "revelation." When confronted, however, with the fact that the Apostle Cephas disagreed with him on one significant issue, Paul could not reply that Cephas was a false apostle, for Paul had previously recognized him to be a genuine apostle. Nevertheless, at a church conference in Galatia, where Cephas and Paul met face to face, Paul charged that Cephas had not acted consistently with the revelation that Cephas himself had previously received from Christ. Indeed, Paul went so far as to say that Cephas had acted *insincerely*! Convinced as he was of the truth and authority of his own revelation, Paul was psychologically so locked into his new belief-system that he seemed unable even to imagine that Cephas could be *sincere* in his *interpretation* of his own revelation *if* that interpretation contradicted Paul's interpretation.

The fundamental point we are making here is this: As is true of religious movements in our time, early Christianity was not lacking in the flow of messages and revelations purporting to be from God. As Professor Howard Clark Kee and others[16] have recently argued, early Christians were charismatics receiving all sorts of visions and voices thought to be direct from the Spirit, Christ, or God. What the Christians lacked was an effective *control mechanism* that would provide a measure of structure and order for the putative revelations. A detailed study of Paul's letters suggests that he himself helped to formulate three of Christianity's control mechanisms.

Paul's Three Control Mechanisms

First, like many charismatic leaders today, Paul made himself and his message central and authoritative. No one can read Paul's letters without encountering a man who would entertain no doubts about his claims about his apostleship and about his "revelations." In fact, to sell himself as a genuine apostle, Paul made use of sometimes questionable rhetorical devices and hurled abusive names and adjectives at his rivals. "Look out for the dogs," he told his Philippian readers (Philippians 3:2 RSV). In

---

[16]See Howard Clark Kee, *Community of the New Age: Studies in Mark's Gospel* (Philadelphia: Westminster Press, 1977), pp. 143, 165, 168; 1 Clement, chapters 59 and 63; Gunther Bornkamm, *Paul*, trans. D. M. G. Stalker (New York: Harper & Row, 1971), p. 71.

opposing those who held that a male Christian convert should first undergo the Jewish rite of circumcision, Paul wrote crudely that he wished that his opponents "would mutilate themselves!" (Galatians 5:12 RSV).

Some of Paul's arguments in defense of his apostleship and the validity of his revelations seem to be irrelevant, particularly in those arguments in which he boasts and then apologizes for boasting. It is necessary, however, to understand what Paul's problem was if we are to understand his seemingly irrelevant arguments. His problem can be stated very simply: He felt it to be imperative to convince his readers and audience of his *sincerity*! By giving accounts of his trials, afflictions and his freely donated labor, Paul hoped to convince his audience of his sincerity. His underlying assumption was that an insincere person would not willingly suffer the abuse and hardship that Paul had suffered. He wore his afflictions and trials as if they were an authenticating badge of genuineness as an apostle.

In contributing to the development of a social mechanism to control the epidemic of revelations among early charismatic Christianity, Paul's first step was to *set forth boldly his own revelations as the rule and standard* by which to judge all other revelations. He did not deny that in the churches there were revelations in addition to his own. His point was that no reputed revelation could be regarded as having the seal of divine authenticity if it contradicted what Paul had preached. Even if an "angel from heaven" should preach a gospel contrary to what Paul had preached, the church should disregard the angel's message (Galatians 1:8).

In our attempt to gain more insight into the structure and development of the conversion process, we have found the Apostle Paul to be a fruitful figure of study since in him we learn of both the conditions under which revelations are generated and the process by which the production of revelations is restrained and directed. There is a second way in which Paul contributed to the development of a mechanism for controlling the outbreak of revelations among early charismatic Christians. He recognized *as binding on himself* the reputed revelations of certain other men who had been accepted as apostles. He acknowledged their revelations, along with his own, as *authoritative and normative*. Once he had recognized Peter to be an apostle, Paul could not believe that his own revelation stood in contradiction to Peter's revelation. At that point, Paul contributed to what later developed into an authoritative scripture or standard revelation for the entire Christian movement. The need for order and control in the churches was to make itself felt among the early Christian charismatics. This need can be detected as early as Paul's own letters and travels.

In order to continue to live while the threat of total chaos stares one in the face, an individual may leap gladly into the arms of a religious movement that promises to save him from the chaos. It is ironic, however, that this same religious movement may find itself facing the threat of chaos, a chaos created by the *uncontrolled proliferation of revelations*. If there is anything more destructive of certain types of religious movements than the absence of revelations, it is the uncontrolled profusion of them. Had the early Christians failed to develop a social thermostat to control the rising heat of charismatic fever and the multiplication of revelations moving off in diverse directions, the movement would have fallen apart.

If a religious movement is to endure and thrive, it must sail between the rocky bank of chaos, on the one side, and the shallow bank of rationalized and institutionalized control, on the other side. An individual can suffer his finitude in the dread of becoming either fragmented beyond all self-identity or deprived of vitality by an oppressive control system. The Apostle Paul seemed to sense the need to avoid both fragmentation and excessive control. Hence, while not allowing himself to disagree with the presumed *revelations* of a fellow Christian apostle, Paul could allow himself to disagree with Peter on a question of *interpretation and application* of Peter's own revelations!

This distinction between revelation and interpretation gave the early Christians a measure of flexibility for handling difficult practical problems without toppling into chaos and total confusion. New converts to a religion are often desperate to have their religion dictate inspired revelations and answers to some of their critical practical problems. As time passes, however, the converts may see that some practical problems are not covered unequivocally by their religion. The distinction between an authoritative revelation and a less authoritative interpretation may be seen in Paul's advice on marriage and divorce. In I Corinthians 7:7, 10-12, Paul himself says that he is giving his own personal judgement since he has received no direct revelation from the Lord on certain questions of marriage, divorce, and remarriage. In I Corinthians 7:40 he says that he thinks he has the Spirit of God when he gives certain pieces of practical advice. But this is different from claiming to have received a direct revelation on the matter. (See I Corinthians 7:25.)

We have said that Paul contributed to the rationalization of the entire conversion process by, first, setting up both himself as an apostle and his revelations as authoritative. His revelations could not be questioned or challenged. Second, he in effect strengthened his authority by aligning himself with Peter and other men who were already accepted by some as genuine apostles with authentic and authoritative revelations. While insisting that he received his revelation "from no man," Paul nevertheless did not isolate himself to the point of setting himself up as the sole recipient of the mystery of Christ revealed from heaven.

We have already discussed what was in effect the third way that Paul contributed to the process of rationalizing the conversion experiences of Christians. We pointed out how he virtually institutionalized the charismatic Christian prophets by requiring them to listen to one another and to, in effect, *reflect* on the voices or revelations coming to them.

The Apostle Paul and the Reverend Moon

A naturalistic inquiry into the dynamics of religious conversion allows us to point out important psychological similarities between Paul and Sun Myung Moon. Both men experienced vivid visions and heard voices which they took to be, not hallucinations, but direct communiques from the deity.

Both Paul and Moon endured considerable persecution, abuse, and severe hardship because of their religious endeavors. And each man interpreted his hardships to be trials or tests of *himself* as a very special agent of God.

Theologian Herbert Richardson contends that the opposition which Moon has received from Christians is motivated largely by an underlying prejudice against Orientals. But Richardson fails to understand that Moon would be regarded in very much the same way as he is now if he were an Anglo-Saxon from Indianapolis and professed to have received divine revelation. Like the Apostle Paul, Moon came to see himself as something of a *chosen person* whose claims to divine relevation simply ought, he thought, to be accepted by others as self-authenticating. Taking what Paul and Moon have revealed about their own private lives, we have concluded that neither of them had seriously raised for himself the question, "Am I perhaps in error to suppose that it was the Lord who spoke to me?" When his voices and visions appeared to him, neither Paul nor Moon seemed to have any psychological mechanism for approaching his voices or revelations with the measure of doubt essential to rational investigation.

This inability to doubt one's voices or to challenge their commands and statements is characteristic of some people today whose "voices" often speak with prime authority. Professor Julian Jaynes raises the crucial

> question of why such voices are believed, why obeyed. For believed as objectively real, they are, and obeyed as objectively real in the face of all the evidence of experience and the mountains of common sense. Indeed, the voices a [schizophrenic] patient hears are more real than the doctor's voice.[17]

---

[17]Jaynes, *The Origin of Consciousness*, pp. 94-95. We do not agree with Jaynes that

Speaking of the "patient" and his voices, Jaynes adds:
That he alone hears the voices is not of much concern.
Sometimes he feels he has been honored by his gift, singled out
by divine forces, elected and glorified, and this even when the
voice reproaches him bitterly . . .[18]

Paul described an experience in which he thought he had been carried into the third or final heaven to hear things not to be related (II Corinthians 12). He could not determine whether he was in or out of his body at the time of the experience. Today, an increasing number of people seem to feel free to speak of having what they interpret to be out-of-body experiences. We will not dwell on the psychological phenomenon of depersonalization, which includes the feeling that one is detached from oneself, sometimes seeing or hearing oneself as another person. If this is the experience that Moon and Paul enjoyed, it is quite likely that each man heard his own voice, that is, a voice or voices coming from his own neural system, which he mistook for the voice of a divine being beyond himself.

According to one study at the University of Newcastle in England, women are more prone to having the experience of so-called self-detachment or depersonalization. It is to be noted that when instructing the prophets at Corinth to gain control of the spirit of prophets, Paul did not allow women to speak in church at all. They were to keep silent (I Corinthians 14:34). According to Acts 2:17, sons and *daughters* shall prophesy. But according to Paul, if the daughters could prophesy at all, they were not to do so in church (I Corinthians 14:34). This heavy-handed mechanism of social control was not invented by Paul, but rather was inherited by him from his worship in the synagogue, where women were forbidden even to read aloud a lesson from Scripture.

For Paul, there is in Christ neither male nor female. But inside the church, the rationalization process had already made it a violation of divine law for the prophetess to prophesy. If she receives revelation, she must keep it to herself until she finds a more reinforcing social setting outside the church.

We noted earlier that Paul did distinguish his thinking process from what he took to be the command or voice of the Lord. It will be interesting to observe how the Reverend Moon will come to interpret his own *Divine Principle.* Currently, he believes that he has received revelations—"ultimate truth"—from God and that some of the revelations are now

---

there is an objective medical condition labeled "schizophrenia." Our point is that visual and auditory hallucinations often figure in putative revelations.

[18]Ibid., p. 95.

contained in *Divine Principle*. But as his disciple and translator Young Oon Kim said to one of us, the Reverend Moon is not satisfied with *Divine Principle*. The key question for the sincere believer in Moon's apostleship is this: Will his future communications to his followers be regarded as divine *revelations*? If the answer is yes, will they be given a higher status than *Divine Principle*? Or will they perhaps be given a lower status—as *interpretations and applications* of the earlier revelation? It is even possible that Moon's putative revelations in the future will supersede some of what is found in *Divine Principle*. Indeed, some of the students at the Unification Theological Seminary are already detecting at least *apparent* contradictions in *Divine Principle*. Moon may find it necessary to receive new revelations to answer problems raised by *Divine Principle*.

Of course, there is the genuine possibility that Sun Myung Moon is no longer hearing voices, no longer having visions of what he regards to be God. If this is happening—and we think there is some reason to believe that it is—then Moon's preaching may become something like cashing checks on an earlier deposit! That is, he must now "remember" and explicate his "revelations" that were received at an earlier time in his life but which have not yet been recorded in *Divine Principle* or anywhere else. Or, taking the rationalization process one step further, he may do what the Mormon president has done, namely, make a decision in light of the crucial problem at hand and simply designate it as a divine revelation. If God works in mysterious ways, prophets demonstrate an ability to work in a variety of ways under a variety of conditions.

The Community and the Sacred Book

Once the voices have lost their powerful authority to move and guide human action, some other authority must be found. In the next chapter, we will inquire into the authority of community and sacred text in generating the individual's second birth and in sustaining the new-born convert. We will also try to show why we have concluded that virtually everyone has been born again, not in a supernatural way, but in a more practical and realistic way. This needs clarification, since it is one of the major points of the book. We will argue that the human individual is the kind of being that is only half born when he or she is delivered from the mother's womb. The social womb must adopt the new biological infant and transform it into a person.

Chapter IV

The Social Womb

Society and Religion: An Interaction

Emile Durkheim, the noted student of the social dimension of religion, in his *The Elementary Forms of Religious Life,*[1] concluded that religion is necessary to the social existence of mankind. If religion is removed, society will come apart. Preachers have of course been saying this for centuries, some even going so far as to insist that their kind of religion alone is necessary. Durkheim turns the coin over and adds that a religion's style and content is largely shaped by a complex background of social forces, institutions, and other social realities. In short, there is an intimate and necessary interrelationship between society and religion. Just as the fetus and the womb that bears it affect each other, so religion and society mutually affect each other. Those who study religion scientifically search for the specific ways in which this interaction proceeds.

Collective Representations

Emile Durkheim was one of the first students of religion to stress the powerful role of what he calls the "collective representations of religion." His point is that through religion society generates certain

---

[1]Trans. J. W. Swain (London: George Allen and Unwin Ltd., 1915).

representations that serve both to inspire and to inform the society or group as a whole. These representations are a collection of socially generated and selected pictures, dreams, key images, analogies, and models that the society forms of itself. It is as if through its religious life the society creates a self-portrait. Religion is society's way of inspiring itself and representing its ideal self to itself.

This self-portrayal, this collective representation, is not composed of descriptive statements alone. It is more on the order of a creative painting than a mere snapshot of itself. The religious model which the community sets forth in portrayal of itself is a statement not only of what the community *is*, but also what it *could* be ideally and even what it *ought* to be. If a society calls itself a fellowship, it is not only portraying itself as a very special community of believers, but also imposing on itself certain imperatives, ideals, dreams, and visions of what could be or even ought to be.

Why should an individual become caught up in this process of collective idealization? Why should anyone even think to be a part of a group's efforts to identify itself as special entity or manifestation in the world? These questions erroneously presuppose that a person has the *choice* of either participating in some social body or remaining outside the social womb. In reality, there can be no *individual* identity apart from social identity. The idea of individuality is itself an idea that the society alone can create for its members to receive as their social inheritance. Even then, different types of societies will produce different styles and images of what individuality means. Just as the biological parents contribute to the biological constitution of their child, so each social body contributes some of its own marks and traits to the children that it adopts.

Apart from the second birth (which takes place in the *social* womb), the human individual would remain a biological mass at best, void of all rights and meaning, having no value and no personhood. This second birth is not a supernatural influx, but rather is the gift of the social unit into which the human organism is adopted. The life of the second birth is not flesh and blood, but rather is the steady flow of stimuli and reinforcements which the social womb literally feeds into the human organism and nervous system.

Many charismatic and evangelical Christians are taught by their social unit to believe that they alone are the truly "born again," that they alone have recevied the second birth. But the underlying theme of this book is that *every human individual who can communicate with words and symbols has been born again*. Except a human organism be born again in the social womb, he will never share in the Kingdom of Personhood.

The Social and Shifty Species

Behold the human species—the most powerful creature on earth! There is no animal on earth that man could not destroy. But we are speaking here, not of men or women as individuals, but of "man" as a collective or a group. The individual has neither the fierce teeth of the baboon, the thick protective skin of the elephant, nor the destructive claws of the tiger or lion. The human species has survived the threats of predators and the uncertainties of nature in general, not because of one *individual's* strength, but because of the *group's* strength. By themselves, human individuals could not have stalked their prey and defended themselves against the more powerful predators. Human individuals had to strive together in groups in order to make it in the world.

But there were other factors at work in human beings. Man's unexcelled brain in the world gave him advantages over all the other animals. By the power of imagination he could leap to new alternatives and new plans of action, whereas other creatures, bound by rigid instincts, were able to continue only in their predetermined ways. When the environment shifted radically, some animals lacked the imagination and flexibility to develop new patterns of behavior and new ways necessary to make it in the world. Lacking flexibility, they died along with their instincts, whereas human beings, with their sensitive brains, could shift their thinking and modify their patterns of behavior sufficiently to adapt to critical environmental changes.

As is often the case, however, an advantage in one direction becomes a disadvantage in another. And so it has been with the shifty, highly flexible brain of the human species. As the French philosopher Henri Bergson noted, mankind's extreme flexibility and plasticity has been both his great strength and a genuine danger for him. The flexibility of human beings gave them the capacity to be shifty in the worst sense of the word. Not only could they shift in times of radical environmental crises, but they could become flexible and shifty to the point of declining in their ability to work and live together as a group. In short, it was quite possible for them to become exceedingly unpredictable, arbitrary, and unreliable—shifty!—in their relationships with one another. But when such unreliability developed beyond a critical point among certain particular human groups and communities, they lost the cohesiveness necessary to their self-defense and survival.

What does all this have to do with religion? The answer is that religion has traditionally functioned as a powerful cohesive force within the human group or community. If human individuals simply *had* to be held together as a group or community in order to survive, then religion seems to have played a crucial—perhaps even necessary—role in that survival of the human species.

Emile Durkheim, the noted French sociologist and philosopher of religion, was one of the first to grasp just how religion functions in a society. We ourselves in this book have stressed that religion is a response to the sense of finitude. Durkheim went on to show that religion has rendered human individuals *less* finite *in fact* by binding each of them together as a social unit. This is not to say that Durkheim thought that religion could eliminate human finitude altogether, but rather that it reduced some *degree* of human weakness. It also overcame some *areas* of their weakness by actually providing them the strength that only participants in the group or community could enjoy.

The Role of Religion to Generate Courage

Our thesis here is not that religions have been a total blessing in every way to mankind. Rather, like Durkheim, we wish to emphasize that in general religion has not been a total curse—as Sigmund Freud sometimes thought. Even though there are many ill effects of religion and some religions do more harm than do others, it is misguided zeal to focus on the evils of religion to the point that religion's profound contributions to human survival itself are overlooked. Doubtless Freud was correct in pointing out that there is neurosis in religion—and, we would even add, something like psychosis.[2] But religion cannot be reduced to nothing but a disease which, like smallpox, should be eliminated wholly from the face of the earth.

We owe Emile Durkheim a great debt for helping us to see that religion has in general served to infuse individuals with the courage to face the world and to venture beyond their fears and deepest anxieties. We take courage for granted, but let a person lose his courage in every dimension of his life and he will perish.

This courage, so essential to the individual's survival, is *generated only within the community!* It is the community, coming together as one cohesive front, that prevents the finite human mortal from becoming altogether demoralized and terrified to the point of becoming incapacitated. It is not quite accurate to say that religion causes individuals to come together for this powerful influx of courage. Rather, religion *is* the coming together of persons as dynamic, supportive, and strengthening "church." The vast differences among the world's religions is primarily the difference in *style* in which each community brings and holds itself

---

[2]See Walter J. Garre, *The Psychotic Animal: A Psychiatrist's Study of Human Delusion* (New York: Human Sciences Press, 1976), chapter 10.

together and works itself up to the level of courage and strength. Songs, rituals, speeches, dances, laying on of hands, stories, dramas, prayers, instructions, pictures, images, masks, exhortations—these are only a few of the means by which each community in its intense religious mode stirs itself to stand against the threatening winds and to serve itself as a thriving "fellowship" or "church."

Religion and the Grandiose

It has frequently been charged that religious stories, theologies, and images have been exceedingly exaggerated and even grandiose in their claims. Unquestionably, this charge has substance. Religion has been accused of projecting images and stories of gods and the like that were wild and fantastic—beyond belief and yet believed.

> Durkheim's point was that societies did indeed project exaggerated representations of themselves, but without such exaggerations the fearful human species quite likely would never have cut for itself a place in nature. By associating together in clans and tribes, preliterate men and women learned that they could build up their courage and strengthen themselves to face life's threats and trials. They learned that only in numbers was greater security possible. Together they were a mighty force, participants of a totem-god. Therefore, *to hold themselves together through the sacred cult became a moral imperative,* that is, a necessity of survival and zestful existence.[3]

In some respects, religion is humanity in its profound social experience of charging itself up for meeting the terrors, threats, and uncertainties of life. It should be no surprise that religious projections and stories have been greatly exaggerated, for they are man's bold and imaginative thrusts back out at the world. Later, we will speak of the element of bluff and serious pretense that men and women express in their religious response to the sense and shock of finitude.

Picture a tribe coming together—a tribe composed of individually finite and powerless creatures. Only together do they become strong and courageous. They bombard one another with exciting stimuli, flood each other with moving stories, and share together rousing exhortations. In some respects, the "rites of passage" that all societies develop serve to give

---

[3]Mary Ann Barnhart, "Religion and Society: A Comparison of Selected Works of Emile Durkheim and Max Weber" (Unpublished M. A. thesis, North Texas State University, Sociology Department, Denton, Texas, 1976), pp. 30-31.

the initiate a glimpse of how terrifying and horrifying life would be without the community. This element of terror in religion needs to be explored further.

Terror in Religion

Many charges have been leveled against various religions, both literate and preliterate religions, because of the terror they generate in individuals. Not just the "primitive" shaman with his grotesque masks, but modern-day Christian evangelists have terrified both children and adults. The evangelists' descriptions of hell are undeniably calculated to strike fear and terror into the hearts of the audience.

Even when the stark terror has been eliminated from religion, still there are many group rituals that are awesome and frightening. But the wisdom of these rituals can be appreciated when we understand that the fright that comes to the individual is experienced *within* the group and under its *control.* In short, even when the religious stories and rituals do disturb and scare their participants, it is within a context of the community's security. The community, which generated the fright artifically, is there to catch the participant before he falls over the cliff. Some religious rituals create an element of *staged terror.* By doing this, the religions sponsoring the rituals give the participant a way of dealing with terror in a more orderly context than he would enjoy if he were forced to face alone the terrors of chaos.

We conjecture that one fundamental reason that the "horror movies" remain popular is that they provide individuals with the opportunity to experience their own reactions to horror and terror within limits. It is pretended horror, and yet the individual's emotional reaction to the staged horror is very real human response and emotion. There is a certain sense of victory and courage generated in the individual who sits through the horror movie and comes out with his sanity intact and his violent emotions mostly under control. He is able to see *in part* what life is at the extreme end of irrationality and chaos. To experience this terror and then to walk away from it into a world of cosmos and even humor is to experience a measure of triumph.

This terrorizing function of religion then, has served in two ways: first, to let the believer practice being scared, frightened, and terrorized—but within the protective circle of the fellowship or church. In the second place religious terror serves to intimidate the individual sufficiently to secure his loyalty to the group. To be sure, religious terror can sometimes become so excessive as to frustrate the group's use of it. In such cases, the individual may take his chances by escaping from the group, although most preliterate tribes did not have this option. But in a society of religious pluralism, the individual, in fleeing the terrors of one religion, often will find another religious community ready to receive him. The tragedy of the People's Temple in Guyana came about to a large extent because its members saw themselves as cut off from all other communities. As they perceived their situation, there was no other social body in which they could find for themselves a plausible and reinforcing self-identity. Jim Jones and their circumstances had conspired to convince them that they had drawn a blank in the lottery of life. In short, the social womb had miscarried.

The Second Birth

The human child is born of two wombs—the motherly womb and the social womb. The womb of his mother's flesh and blood is unique, for it is there that the genes and biological constitution of the new life take their very special form and shape. When the child leaves his secure first womb, he is delivered immediately into the second womb—the social or communal womb. If he is a fortunate infant, this new setting will provide not only food for his stomach but strokes and constructive social messages for his little body and brain.

In the third chapter of the Gospel of John, Jesus is reported to have said the following:

> Truly, truly, I say to you, unless one is born anew, he cannot see the kingdom of God ... Truly, truly, I say to you, unless one is born of water and the Spirit, he cannot enter the kingdom of God. That which is born of flesh is flesh, and that which is born of Spirit is spirit (John 3:3, 5 RSV).

Christians have for centuries been debating the question of what it means to be "born of water." Other religions and cultures have a different idiom in which to express the precise means for obtaining the new birth as they perceive it. By contrast, we wish to focus on the distinction between being "born of flesh" and being "born of Spirit," for it suggests our thesis of the two wombs.

Society is not flesh and blood alone; in addition it brings to flesh and blood the special creative elements by which the human infant over a period of months and years is transformed into a member of the Kingdom of Personhood. Early Christians such as Ambrose and Augustine insisted that apart from the Church, there can be no salvation. But a revised version of this view would read as follows: Apart from the social womb, the individual can never become a person with special rights, experiences, privileges, and responsibilities.

The covenant between the individual and his community is the bond by which the tiny creature of flesh and blood is gradually transformed from a purely natural creature to a "new creation." The community says to him, "You must be created anew, born again." The social womb slowly "regenerates" him, transforms him, and "saves" him from remaining a mere organism governed by the laws of chemistry and biology alone. The phrase *the social construction of reality* is most appropriate when we are discussing the individual's second birth. The helpless infant which raw nature alone has deposited into the social womb is neither a completed animal nor yet a person, but a potential person who must continue to develop until the social womb molds him into a participating and more or less responsible member of the community.[4]

The testimony of individuals being "converted" from this or that way of life to another way is ultimately a testimony to the power of the society or community to give shape and direction to the individual lives that are nourished within it. The essentially religious person knows that he is not his own creator in every respect. He does not fancy himself to be "self-made," but rather to be the fortunate heir of something beyond himself. For many people, this "something" is a special infusion of grace coming from beyond the individual's own limited resources. Emile Durkheim reasoned that the individual's society or community is the true source of this special grace of acceptance and nourishment. This does not mean that society is a cosmic and infallible deity, but rather is more enduring than the individual and in some profound sense transcends him. For Durkheim, the Kingdom of Heaven is in reality the Kingdom of Society, both as society actually exists and as it might become. No one enters this sacred Kingdom to become a responsible member until he is born again in accord with the requirements institutionalized by the particular society in which he has been nourished.[5]

The American philosopher John Dewey had a profound appreciation of the fact that the gifts of the community to the individual are a matter of unearned "grace."

> We who now live are parts of a humanity that extends into the remote past; a humanity that has interacted with nature. The things in civilization we most prize are not of ourselves. They exist by grace of the doings and sufferings of the continuous human community in which we are a link.[6]

---

[4]See Cliff Edwards, *Biblical Christian Marriage* (Atlanta: John Knox Press, 1977), chapter 3.

[5]See Emile Durkheim, *The Elementary Forms of the Religious Life*, p. 447.

[6]John Dewey, *A Common Faith* (New Haven: Yale University Press, 1934), p. 87.

The Discovery of Society

Theologians have spoken at length of the mysterious and invisible ways of God. For Durkheim, the ways of society have often seemed beyond comprehension. Only slowly are students of society and culture beginning to examine the previously invisible and mysterious hand of society, a hand which eventually molds and shapes the once-born infant into a twice-born person. Even when we cannot see the moon at noon, we have reason to believe that it exerts considerable influence on the earth. Similarly, there are many social and cultural forces which are shaping and transforming people's lives in countless ways even when they are unaware of these forces.

When Galileo looked through his telescope, he observed that the heavens were riddled with countless more stars than he and his contemporaries had even begun to imagine. Members of the Inquisition refused to believe that such a vast number of stars existed. When Darwin and his followers showed that the ancestral roots of human life on earth reach back well over a million years, he met fierce opposition from those who had been convinced that the universe was only five thousand years old. Today, the discovery of the social womb with its vast and complex array of patterns, structures, variables, and forces has scarcely created a stir among the masses of people, for they are as yet unable to comprehend the intricate and complex working of the social womb. In their book *The Discovery of Society,* Randall Collins and Michael Makowsky point out that such students of society and culture as Emile Durkheim, Max Weber, or George Herbert Mead are hardly known outside the circle of a few behavioral scientists and philosophers.[7]

Thanks to the sciences of embryology and genetics, as well as other recently maturing sciences, the growth and development of the fetus inside the mother's womb is now understood more thoroughly than it was even twenty years ago. The birth of an infant is no longer regarded as an incomprehensible mystery, although there is still much to learn about it. Similarly, the process by which the second womb—the social womb—brings about the individual's second birth, while still under a cloud of mystery and confusion for many people, is nevertheless coming gradually to be better understood. Being "born again" is to be seen, not as an entirely mysterious work, but as the work of deep and profound social conditions, forces, patterns, and causes to be included under the heading of *the social womb.* Students of society and religion are now in better position to study

---

[7](New York: Random House, 1972), pp. 12-14.

more systematically the ways in which the social womb converts its new subjects into participating members of the community.

The New Birth as a Universal Phenomenon

The mere fact that most if not all individuals have no clear and distinct memories of their physical birth from their mother's womb is hardly a basis for denying that they were born. Similarly, a person may have been "born again" even though he has no clear and distinct memory of his new birth process. We contend that *every socialized human being has been born again*. To be sure, various cultures and groups have their own special idiom in which they formulate and express the second birth process, but no culture or group can sustain itself without institutionalizing this process and inculcating it into the lives of each new generation.

Our main criticism of the evangelical and charismatic account of the new birth process is that by speaking mystically of supernatural causes, it draws attention away from many of the real social and cultural causes. The hypothesis of supernaturalism creates a fog which makes it difficult for many people to detect and study carefully some of the rich and complex social causes and conditions that have shaped their lives both for good and ill.

Freely You Have Received

Many people do not recall when they learned to speak their native tongue. Yet they speak it daily and with ease. Learning the language is itself a part of the new birth process. Traditionally, many religions have held that the new birth comes, not because the recipient deserves it, but because the deity wills to bestow it. In our terminology, the community or society "wills" to bestow on its new infants the gift of language as well as countless other gifts. But, having received the gifts and values freely, the individual becomes responsible to the society and to those who come after him. In John Dewey's words,

> Ours is the responsibility of conserving, transmitting, rectifying and expanding the heritage of values we have received that those who come after us may receive it more solid and secure, more widely accessible and more generously shared than we have received it.[8]

In biblical terms, "freely ye have received, freely give" (Matthew 10:8 KJV).

---

[8]John Dewey, *A Common Faith*, p. 87

Pluralism

The new birth or conversion of the individual is a form of induction into full membership of the group. In some societies, the transition and transformation are simpler than in others. In contemporary society, the new birth process is complicated by the fact that society in general is composed of numerous subsocieties or subgroups. Furthermore, some of these subgroups stand in rivalry with one another. Hence, it is possible to be converted from one religious community to another. Jehovah's Witnesses are composed of a number of former Methodists, Baptists, Catholics, and the like. These people regard themselves as having been *converted* from their former allegiance. In a highly pluralistic society such as the United States, religious freedom means the right to convert others, or to be converted, from one religious community to another.

Each religious group has its own special induction procedures and requirements, as well as its own special beliefs, values, and moral imperatives. Kai Nielsen is probably correct to note the vast differences between fundamentalist Christians, on the one hand, and other Christians and Humanists, on the other hand. It is as if the differences were between two tribes or two distinct ages in history.[9]

Nevertheless, the variety of distinct religions in, say, the United States and much of Europe and Canada do hold certain values and moral imperatives in common. This is true despite their profound disagreements on a number of points. Each religion in the United States accepts as a moral rule that it will not steal money from the others or interrupt the meetings of the others. Indeed, American society as a whole has a large body of moral rules, regulations, and principles which are held in common by virtually all the members of the various and diverse religions.

This condition of mutual toleration, responsible citizenship toward one another, and willingness to abide by common agreements did not always exist in either Europe or the United States. Roger Williams, the seventeenth century Baptist, was exiled from New England because of his religious beliefs, including the belief in religious liberty. Some Quakers and Baptists in England in the same century were jailed because of their religious beliefs and practices. It required centuries for the moral principle of religious liberty to develop and to become eventually the law of the land.

Many sermons have been preached on the influence that religion has had on the improvement and maintenance of society's morality. But it is also true that society has often influenced religion to reform itself. It is

---

[9]See Kai Nielsen, "Religiosity and Powerlessness," *The Humanist*, 37:3 (May/June 1977), 46-48.

often forgotten that sometimes a religion needs a new birth or even a traumatic transformation. In the next chapter we will consider how society and culture determine to a large extent the style and content of the individual's conversion process. But before turning to that chapter, we will summarize the major theme of this chapter.

Summary

Far from being the product of a supernatural infusion or injection, the new birth is a process begun when the biological endowment of the infant first encounters the infusion of social and cultural stimuli and reinforcers. If the human being learns to live outside his mother's womb, it is partly because he now has a social womb in which to live.

The individual must learn to live outside his mother's biological womb, but he cannot live outside the new social womb. It is the social womb that prevents him from becoming totally mad and destroyed by the terror of chaos and finitude shock.

This does not mean, however, that the individual must remain forever within the social womb into which he was delivered at the time of his biological birth. It means, rather, that he must always live inside *some* social womb. He may be delivered from a particular social womb, but if he is, he will have to be adopted into another in order to retain any trace of personal identity.

Later, we will show how it is possible to be "born again" several times, a point which evangelicals have been unable to appreciate. We will also deal later with the myth of individualism (in contrast to individuality). The myth of individualism is dangerous to religious life and human life in general because it begins with the assumption that a vital person can become independent of any and every social womb.

We now turn to consider the question of how the social womb itself works in shaping its adopted sons and daughters. There is no neutral social womb. The one that a person is adopted into makes a profound difference in who he becomes and how he will perceive himself, his rights, and his responsibilities.

Chapter V

The New Birth in Cultural Perspective

Basic Religious Questions in a Pluralistic Society

A pluralistic society provides at least one outstanding advantage that a strict tribal society does not. It is the advantage of providing a number of religious options to choose from. In a pluralistic society, a person is less a prisoner of the view he happened to grow up with. Up to a point at least, he can give up some of the view he inherited and can embrace another view.

But to have this freedom of alternative views is also to have the responsibility of choosing wisely. To face the religious alternatives is also to face the question of which one of them is nearer the truth. Suffering a measure of cognitive or intellectual finitude, the individual in a pluralistic society will very likely find himself asking, "What *can* I believe? What *should* I believe? If I convert to one of the alternative views, which one should it be? Should I remain where I am? If so, why?"

In an effort to deal with these disturbing questions, evangelical and fundamentalist Christians came to believe that no answer could be found through human reason and inquiry alone. That is, human mortals could not answer the questions in any satisfying way. Having come to this conclusion of skepticism, evengelicals and fundamentalists then went on to say that, fortunately, the answers have been revealed in the Bible.

Unfortunately, fundamentalists and evangelicals failed to take seriously the fact that there are other putative Scriptures in the world—the

Qur'an, the Upanishads, the Gita, the Brahmasutras, the Book of Mormon, as well as ancient traditions that are regarded by millions of people to be sacred deposits of truth and instruction. Hence, the individual is faced with two new questions, "Among all these Scriptures and sacred traditions, which one contains the revelation of truth? Should I regard *any* of them to be a wholly reliable revelation?"

Fundamentalists and evangelicals find that they are thrown back, after all, on human reason. First, they are forced to use human reason when attempting to justify their assumption that there absolutely must be a perfect Scripture or revelation somewhere. Second, they are forced to use human reason when trying to justify their choice of *one* Scripture or tradition in preference to the others. It is probably significant that people who embrace a Scripture as divine revelation tend to embrace the one that is prevalent in the part of the world in which they grew up. Only a few people in Indianapolis embrace the Upanishads as their sacred text, and very few people in Bombay embrace the Book of Mormon.

Within the Sphere of Thought

Persons who accept one of the Scriptures of the world as the only authoritative revelation of truth tend to underplay the truism that every alleged revelation is embodied in a finite human language. They tend to overlook the fact that a language is a facet of an entire culture and reflects much of the general sphere of thought of which it is a part. Hence, any doctrine or dogma that is said to be revealed in sacred Scripture will likely be colored by its cultural, social, and historical setting. As the philosopher A. N. Whitehead noted,

> No idea is determinate in a vacuum. It has its being as one of a system of ideas. A dogma is the expression of a fact as it appears within a certain sphere of thought. You cannot convey a dogma by merely translating the words; you must also understand the system of thought to which it is relevant.[1]

Most Christians will agree that "the biblical message has to be put back into its own historical setting."[2] The far-reaching implications of this point need to be explored further, since it has an important bearing on the theme of religious conversion or the new birth.

---

[1] A. N. Whitehead, *Religion in the Making* (New York: Living Age Books, Meridian Books, Inc., 1960), p. 125.

[2] René Pache, *The Inspiration and Authority of Scripture*, trans. Helen I. Needham (Chicago: Moody Press, 1969), p. 125.

Historical Relativism

To acknowledge that an alleged piece of revelation of truth must be understood in its historical context is to concede that it is historically limited. That is precisely why the early Christians had to produce the *New* Testament. It was in part to supplement and fulfill the *Old* Testament as they perceived it. But this leaves open the question of whether the New Testament is now to be interpreted in its historical—and therefore limited—setting. It would seem that even the meaning of key Christian terminology is relative to the historical and cultural time of the first century A.D. at least.

There is still another crucial point to be made on this subject. Each historical period—whether the first century A.D. or the sixth century B.C.—will itself have a still wider historical context. In other words, the first century A.D. did not develop in a vacuum. It came out of an even wider cultural context and a still more ancient historical background. Which raises the question of just where to draw the line in saying what is or is not the proper historical and cultural context for an authoritative understanding of a given religious teaching or doctrine. If we reduce the territory of the context, then the meaning of the key religious concepts will be different from what they would be if the circle of context is much wider, or, by contrast, is exceedingly narrow.[3]

This point has been expressed in part by A. N. Whitehead:

> You cannot claim absolute finality for a dogma without claiming a commensurate finality for the sphere of thought within which it arose . . .
>
> A dogma—in the sense of a precise statement—can never be final.[4]

Evangelicals believe that they differ with fundamentalists on at least one crucial point. The former insist that no one passage of the Bible can be properly understood unless it is interpreted in light of the *whole* Bible.[5] Evangelical scholar Bernard Ramm refers to this as "the total web of revelation and redemption."[6] But this total web turns out to be only a web within a larger web, or a web interlaced with countless other webs. In

---

[3]See Ernest Gellner, "Concepts and Society," in Bryan R. Wilson, ed., *Rationality: Key Concepts in the Social Sciences* (New York: Harper & Row, 1970), pp. 18-49.

[4]Whitehead, *Religion in the Making*, p. 126.

[5]See Pache, *The Inspiration and Authority of Scripture*, p. 126.

[6]Bernard Ramm, *Special Revelation and the Word of God* (Grand Rapids: Eerdmans Press, 1961), p. 96.

a somewhat desperate attempt to get out of the web of historical and cultural relativism, Ramm projected the idea of the organic unity of the Bible. But this "organic unity" turns out to be little more than another phrase for the infallible context or unity of all the sub-unities that Ramm believed he had discovered in the Bible. Ramm evidently has not yet seen that the alleged infallible unity of the Bible is pulled apart by two sources that exist in his own sphere of thought. The two sources are (1) the sub-unities within the Bible (each competing for its position of influence) and (2) the wider unity of the mind of God (which, says Ramm, is the supreme unity and context).[7]

In order not to get trapped by one of the sub-unities of the Bible, Ramm provided in good evangelical tradition a principle of flexibility. It is the principle of "progressive revelation." With it, Ramm hoped to keep the swarm of sub-unities in their proper place. What he failed to understand, however, is that the notion of "progressive revelation" is merely a theological phrase for the idea of *historical relativism*. It is a notorious fact that Christians have for centuries taken the principle of progressive revelation as a device for controlling rival interpretations of the mind of God. Professor Ramm, deeply disturbed by the obvious existence of relativism among evangelicals, wrote the little book *Patterns of Religious Authority*[8] in an attempt to counter this relativism. In this book Ramm anticipated the current charismatics, who seek to consult directly the mind of God (via the Holy Spirit). Ramm himself conceded that since the Bible does not provide a systematic theology, the element of *interpretation* is still necessary to produce systematic theology.[9] It is both enlightening and significant that the adherents of one version of systematic theology will charge that the rival theologies have not paid sufficient attention to the *historical context*. Our conclusion regarding this fascinating debate among evangelicals is that the situation is so critical that no clear agreement—beyond the mere slogan "the whole Bible"—has been reached as to what is the full and proper circle of context for interpreting even the most crucial passages of the Bible.

Cultural Relativism

One evangelical, E. J. Carnell, argued that Paul's commandment, "Greet one another with a holy kiss" (Romans 16:16 RSV) is culturally relative and not binding on contemporary Christians.[10] On this question of cultural

---

[7]See ibid., pp. 100-105.

[8](Grand Rapids: Eerdmans, 1957).

[9]Ibid., p. 98, fn. 14.

[10]See E. J. Carnell, *The Case for Orthodox Theology* (Philadelphia: Westminster, 1959), p. 63.

relativism, Carnell went on to say the following:

> Peter tells women how to adorn themselves; and his advice is
> remarkably precise: "Let not yours be the outward adorning
> with braiding of hair, decoration of gold, and wearing of robes"
> (I Peter 3:3 RSV). When enthusiasts cite this passage to control
> women's fashions, they render Christianity trivial and
> offensive. The apostles taught the principle of modesty
> through counsel which was pertinent to the *culture of that day*.
> In *another culture* a woman might *prove* her modesty by
> braided hair, decoration of gold, and wearing of robes.[11]

With statements like this, Carnell stirred up a hornet's nest among
evangelicals and fundamentalists. He offered what he thought were
reasonable rules or principles of interpretation. In effect, he brought up
the old and thorny question of where to draw the line in disregarding the
cultural limits of the sacred text. To be sure, every book has the problem of
how to interpret and apply it. But evangelicals and fundamentalists
sometimes have the added problem of having their eternal salvation to
ride on the Scriptural interpretations that they select. Furthermore, they
speak boldly of an *infallible* revelation, which immediately becomes
diluted by human interpretation.

The different styles of conversion or of the new birth found among
Christians are to be explained in part by the fact that after almost two
thousand years, Christians still have a deep and profound disagreement
among themselves as to how Scripture is to be interpreted on various
cultural matters. Indeed, if, as Carnell and others say, some passages are
merely "local" and "relative" regarding what women shall, wear or
whether Christians should kiss, the question emerges as to whether some
of the *theological* opinions of Paul and Peter are perhaps historically and
culturally relative, also. If they are relative, then are they binding on
contemporary believers? In his provocative book *Ethics in the New
Testament*, Professor Jack T. Sanders wrestled with this very issue. What
this New Testament scholar concluded is as follows:

> The ethical positions of the New Testament are the children of
> their own times and places, alien and foreign to this day and age.
> . . . We are freed from bondage to that tradition, and we are
> able to propose, with the author of the Epistle of James, that
> tradition and precedent must not be allowed to stand in the
> way of what is humane and right.[12]

---

[11]Ibid., p. 61. Italics added except for the word "prove."

[12]Jack T. Sanders, *Ethics in the New Testament: Change and Development*
(Philadelphia: Fortress Press, 1975), p. 130.

It appears doubtful that any evangelical or fundamentalist Christian could accept this conclusion without being converted to another religion or at least to another form of Christianity radically different from his own version.

When it is revealed by various polls that a number of Protestants claim to be "born again," we hope that our readers will appreciate the diversity of opinion as to what is entailed in the phrase "born again." Pluralism among Christians alone is alive and thriving.[13]

The Voice of the Authority Figure

In the previous chapter we presented the theory that up until roughly three thousand years ago, human individuals quite normally and regularly heard voices that instructed them in what to do, especially in situations of personal stress and crisis. What we could not deal with in the previous chapter was the question of the great diversity of opinion regarding what the voices commanded and how they were identified. In some societies, the source was regarded to be the father; for others it was the voice of the king or of the god.

Professor Julian Jaynes draws upon research in archeology, linguistics, biology, and other disciplines to conclude that for a million years or more the human species had no need for voices (auditory hallucinations), since human beings traveled in small hunting-gathering groups, each of about twenty to thirty members. Had the group been much larger than that, it would have ceased to enjoy an effective flow of communication required to render the group able both to protect and feed itself, as well as to raise its young.[14]

For a million years *homo sapiens* did not have a very complex language, which is probably why their tools were very simple and limited. Most of what was learned from generation to generation was learned, not by oral instruction, but by imitation—which is the way bicycle riding is usually learned today.

But there seems to have been an explosion of new types of tools from 40,000 B.C. to 25,000 B.C., and Professor Jaynes argues that this creative

---

[13]For a study of the diversity of opinion solely among evangelicals regarding the nature of the Bible, see Stephen T. Davis, *The Debate About the Bible: Inerrancy Versus Infallibility* (Philadelphia: Westminster, 1977). The provocative book by Dewey Beegle, entitled *Scripture, Tradition, and Infallibility* (Grand Rapids: Eerdmans, 1973) raises some very penetrative questions for his fellow evangelicals when he compares the doctrine of the Bible's infallibility with the doctrine of the Pope's infallibility.

[14]See Jaynes, *The Origin of Consciousness*, pp. 127, 129.

breakthrough was facilitated by the emergence of intentional calls, modifiers, and vocal commands that had evolved in the primitive human language. At roughly 25,000 B.C. the emergence of nouns coincided with the drawing of animals on the walls of caves or on horn implements.

When nouns for things developed as a part of human language, the stage was set for "the invention of pottery, pendants, ornaments, and barbed harpoons and spearheads, the last two tremendously important in spreading the human species into more difficult climates."[15] The development of names is conjectured by Jaynes to be about 10,000 B.C. to 8,000 B.C. During this period ceremonial graves became common, which means that when a person died, his name could live on.[16]

If, as Professor Jaynes argues, human beings around 10,000 B.C. began to bury their dead ceremoniously and had names for their departed ancestors, it is quite possible that individuals heard voices which they attributed to their departed ancestors. Before the evolution of conscious self-identity (as we think of it today), the human individual was unable to tell himself consciously how to work in the field or to guide his life. But he could hear a voice, which he took to be that of his father, king, or some other authority figure. And when the authority figure died, the voice did not die inside the head of the survivor but continued to speak. Furthermore, the survivor's *relationship* with the voice continued. Verbal hallucinations may very well have contributed toward the evolution of belief in god or gods. The god was the father or king whose voice lived on after death. In short, the father-god continued to exert influence even after the father or ruler had died.

Even today some transactional analysis therapists speak of the *parent tape* that most individuals in our culture "hear," not overtly but covertly. Indeed, parents sometimes have been surprised to hear themselves utter statements that they had heard their own parents utter many years earlier. Adults sometimes catch themselves thinking a train of thoughts that their parents had spoken years earlier on various occasions.

Of course, most of us today recognize that we are influenced by the *impact* that our parents made on us. If they are dead, we do not think that our parents are still present with us to give us advice and instruction. However, thousands of centuries ago human beings did think that their departed ancestors really were present with them. They did hear voices which they unhesitatingly identified as the voices of parents or authority

---

[15]Ibid., p. 134.

[16]See ibid., 134-36.

figures. Whereas we today may catch ourselves uttering or thinking our deceased parents' words, human beings about 10,000 years ago could hear the commanding voice of the authority figure even though he was no longer alive and even though the words were not necessarily uttered through the survivors' own lips. To be sure, the voice was not literally that of the authority figure but rather was a product of the mechanism of the survivors' brains. Bicameral men and women had no way of knowing that the voices they heard originated from within their own heads.

The Messages of the Voices

There is a bewildering and rich diversity of practices and styles among human societies. One tribe constructs its dwellings in one way; another tribe constructs in another way. One society favors one kind of building material, whereas another society may have no use for the material at all. This means that the building *directions and instructions* that are passed on from one generation to another may vary radically from one society to another. Furthermore, instructions in how to marry properly, how to relate to kin, how to herd animals or plant seeds, how to play, how to talk to one's neighbors, how to paint one's face—all these how-to-do-it instructions vary profoundly from society to society.

Therefore, if parents and authority figures thousands of years ago gave instruction in these and many more such activities, then it is to be expected that the auditory hallucinations that people heard and obeyed varied considerably from society to society. And if the "voices" were taken to be those of the father-gods or king-gods living on forever, then we have already some clue as to how differences among religions came about. Very simply, the "voices" were taken to be divine instructions, commands, and exhortations. The differences between the putative divine messages reflect the different social and cultural settings from which they sprang. Each god spoke in his own cultural dialect.

Diverse Rites of Passage

Each society, with its own slowly-evolved tradition, instructed and still instructs its new members in the procedures for moving through the different stages of their social existence. In his influential book *The Rites of Passage,* Arnold van Gennep points out that in some tribes the novice is considered dead. This stage of "social death" may last for a moderately long time, during which the initiate may be weakened physically and mentally so that he loses most of the recollections of his childhood. After this stage comes to an end, new training and instruction are given to him, and he is also exposed to a variety of ceremonies, new myths, and new recitations.

Some part of his body may be permanently altered—for example, a tooth extracted or some degree of circumcision—to mark the youth off as no longer a youth but an adult member of the tribe. In those tribes in which the novice is considered dead, he will be "resurrected" by some ancient ceremony. He may be required to bathe in a sacred stream, to speak in a special language, or eat special food. "The purpose is to make the novice 'die', to make him forget his former personality and his former world."[17] At this point Christians may be reminded of the sixth chapter of Romans, in which Paul speaks of the new convert's spiritual death and resurrection, and of baptism as an initiation ceremony through which the candidate becomes a resurrected member of the body of Christ.

The point that we wish to stress here, and which Arnold van Gennep also stresses, is that the rites of passage sometimes vary extremely in detail from religion to religion, or from one community to another. Each group tends to regard as quite natural its own ceremonies and procedures for bringing about the candidate's "new birth." The ceremonies and rites that are practiced in other societies are likely to be looked upon as humorous at best, and abominable at worst. Marcus Aurelius, in so many ways a gentle and understanding man, genuinely believed that the Christians in the Roman empire during the second century were a serious threat to the security of the empire. The stories of the ceremonies and rites of the Christians had been so misunderstood by the general population that Marcus Aurelius thought Christians to be weird and perverted to the point of being subversive. Ironically, in times past, Christian missionaries, going into societies that were altogether strange to them, concluded that the native religious ceremonies were abhorrent.

The fourth chapter of Exodus provides an ancient story of an hallucination in which the deity threatened and terrorized a man to the point that he feared that he was going to be killed by the deity. Fortunately, the man's wife was able to discern what the deity was angry about. Apparently, the foreskin of her son had not been removed. "Then Zipporah took a flint [a very primitive tool] and cut off her son's foreskin, and touched Moses' feet with it, and said, 'Surely you are a bridegroom of blood to me!' So he [i.e., the deity] let him alone" (Exodus 4:25-26 RSV).

Earlier in this fourth chapter of Exodus, the deity—Yahweh—explains that Aaron will be a mouth for Moses, who in turn "shall be to him a God" (Exodus 4:16 RSV; italics added). We believe that this is a most revealing passage, for here the word God means very simply the voice of

---

[17]Arnold van Gennep. *The Rites of Passage*, trans. M. A. Vizedom and G. L. Caffee (Chicago: University of Chicago Press, 1960), pp. 75, 81.

instruction and direction! Each Egyptian king regarded himself to be the agent for repeating the voice of the previous king, who was also considered to be a god. The voice of a king-god could continue after his death and "be" the guiding voice of the next king-god.[18]

> Osiris . . . was not a "dying god" . . . He was the hallucinated voice of a dead king whose admonitions could still carry weight. And since he could still be heard, there is no paradox in the fact that the body from which the voice once came should be mummified, with all the equipment of the tomb providing life's necessities: food, drink, slaves, women, and the lot. There was no mysterious power that emanated from him; simply his remembered voice which appeared in hallucination to those who had known him and which could admonish or suggest even as it had before he stopped moving and breathing . . . Further, the relationship between Horus and Osiris, "embodied" in each new king and his dead father forever, can only be understood as the assimilation of an hallucinated advising voice into the king's own voice, which then would be repeated with the next generation.[19]

The Message of the God

To be sure, the dead father-king-god whose "voice" was heard by his successor king-god did not really speak but rather was hallucinated. Furthermore, *what* the "voice" commanded and advised was not something that the dead father-king-god had discerned with his own brain, since that brain had ceased to function. Rather, the *living* king's brain produced the voice. It was he whose senses received the input from what was going on in his kingdom about him. It was he who listened to the counsel of finance ministers, military officers, priests, and others of the court. And then it was he who unconsciously made the decision which was formulated by his brain and transformed into the hallucinated "voice." Needless to say, the previous decisions of the previous king-gods were taken into consideration, just as judges today take into consideration the decisions and opinions of previous judges. In this sense the "voice" of the dead still speaks in our time as well as in the time of the Egyptian king-gods. The difference is that each surviving king hallucinated and heard a voice which he took to be that of the father-king-god before him. And so the dead lived on, and the traditions of the past were continued, not

---

[18]See Jaynes, *The Origin of Consciousness*, p. 187.

[19]Ibid.

slavishly, but effectively as the living king endeavored to apply the tradition that he had received to new circumstances and situations.

This simply means that each culture—not just the Egyptian culture— had its own tradition which had developed over many years. The commands of the gods in every culture were commands rising out of the tradition and experiences of the society to which the gods belonged.[20] The "God of Israel" did not give commands out of the tradition of another people. Indeed, the rivalry among the gods is in reality the conflict among societies or cultures. The Hebrews (Khabiru) were a people with a developing subculture of their own. The least that we can say is that the Hebrews were a scattered people who, because of their social situation, had enough in common, enough mutual support, to bring about the formation of a reasonably strong Hebrew nation at a time when the Egyptians on the west and the Mesopotamians on the east were uncharacteristically weak in military and economic power. Like their neighbors, the Hebrews produced their own versions of their own God.

The moral development within the Hebrew concepts of God reflects the moral development of the Hebrews themselves as a people. Or, stated more succinctly, the commands and moral injunctions that the Hebrew God gave to his people were in reality the commands and injunctions that the Hebrews were attempting to give themselves. The voice of God is the collective conscience of the people when they perceive themselves as an idealized whole.

Social Sources of Theology

Biblical scholars are keen to point out radical differences between the Bible and other Scriptures of the world. What they sometimes fail to stress is that each Scripture is unique. But the mere fact of a Scripture's uniqueness tells us nothing in favor of its divine origin. After devoting years to the study of five great world religions, Max Weber concluded that the sacred Scriptures of the world are so radically different because behind them had been economic, linguistic, ideological, class, political, and other sociocultural forces and conditions. It was this massive build-up of each sociocultural pattern that helped to shape, color, and give rise to its sacred Scripture. If Weber's study of the major religions of the world means anything, it is that their sacred Scriptures were not all saying the same thing. There are fundamental and irreconcilable differences among these Scriptures of the world, and it has been the sociocultural differences of peoples which have made this diversity of Scriptures a fact. Weber

---

[20]See Max Weber, *The Sociology of Religion*, pp. 35, 68.

goes on to say that the diversity and changes within a single sacred Scripture—for example, the Bible—can be explained only by political, social, economic, and other such changes in Hebrew history and early Christian history. No profound understanding of a charismatic movement or a "born again" phenomenon can be had unless the relevant social, political, economic, and general cultural circumstances are taken into consideration. For example, it is very likely that there is some left-out "class" in America that is using the "born again" phenomenon to gain for itself some political and economic advantage in the land. Weber notes that "classes with high social and economic privilege will scarcely be prone to evolve the idea of salvation. Rather they assign to religion the primary function of their own life pattern and situation in the world."[21]

This is not to say that the "born again" phenomenon can be reduced to a political move or that its participants see themselves as an emerging political bloc. Rather, it is to say that the religious conversion is often more than what both its defenders and its opponents have sometimes admitted.

We contend that Durkheim and Weber are correct to conclude that the personality of the gods varies with the many facets of the society in which the idea of each god was gradually conceived and shaped.[22] Old Testament scholars are fond of noting that the God of the Old Testament created the world out of nothing. But if Weber and Durkheim are correct in their conjectures, the idea of a God creating out of nothing was hardly an idea created out of nothing. According to Weber,

> the regulation of the Nile was the source of the Egyptian monarch's strength. In the desert and semiarid regions of the Near East this control of irrigation waters was indeed *one source of the conception of a god who had created the earth and man out of nothing* and not merely fashioned them, as was believed elsewhere. A riparian economy of this kind actually did produce a harvest out of nothing, from the desert sands.[23]

In an ingenious article entitled "Iknaton: The Great Man *vs.* the Culture Process," anthropologist L.A. White shows how an Egyptian king's monotheism developed out of the Egyptian tradition rather than as a sudden revelation out of the blue.[24] Durkheim contends that when a tribe

---

[21]Ibid., p. 107.

[22]See ibid., p. 10.

[23]Ibid., p. 57. Italics added.

[24]See L. A. White, *The Science of Culture: A Study of Man and Civilization* (New York: Farrar, Straus and Giroux, 1949), chapter 9.

acquired "a livelier sentiment of itself," it tended to "incarnate its sentiment into some personage who became its symbol."[25] We would go so far as to say that the morality of a group is reflected in its theology and its concept of the deity. The fires of hell in some theologies are in reality the reflection of the rage and resentment burning in the hearts of believers whose compassion is still retarded by a vindictive ideology. However, some generations of believers have inherited a theology that reflects more the face of their ancestors than of themselves.

Moral Transcendence

In his massive and controversial *Sociobiology: The New Synthesis,* zoologist Edward O. Wilson of Harvard University writes, "Human beings are absurdly easy to indoctrinate—they *seek* it."[26] Another way of saying this is that when the human infant leaves his mother's womb, he is only half made. His endowment of instincts is sufficient to allow him to select certain social relationships in preference to other reinforcers. But he has no instincts that compel him to act morally. What we can say is that given enough time and a reasonably efficient system of supports, he will adopt certain patterns of behavior, some of which will be defined by his society as *moral* behavior.

It is very difficult to say that the human infant is "naturally" anything on the moral scale. He is not naturally good; nor is he naturally evil. He is just there with the potentiality for becoming a participating member of his society or for becoming a villain. Indeed, he has the capacity for eventually becoming a loyal and faithful member of a villainous society.

The reason it is so difficult to say that any overt behavior of human beings is "natural" is that the human species is a *social* species. Perhaps that is one of the most natural things that can be said of it.

To be more precise, human life depends on some sort of external structure or culture to give it guidance and direction. In the process of evolving, the human species seems to have lost much of its instinctive endowment in exchange for its intelligence and flexibility. In compensation for the loss of instincts inside the body, humanity adopted social rules and regulations existing outside the body in what anthropologists call "culture." For human beings, rigid instincts have given way to social norms, social habits, social roles, and social structures. According to Henri Bergson, when examined from one standpoint, human

---

[25] Durkheim, *The Elementary Forms*, p. 293.

[26] (Cambridge, Mass.: Belknap Press of Harvard University Press, 1975), p. 562.

social life appears to us a system of more or less deeply rooted habits, corresponding to the needs of the community. Some of them are habits of command, most of them are habits of obedience; whether we obey a person commanding by virtue of a mandate from society, or whether from society itself, vaguely perceived or felt, there emanates an impersonal imperative. Each of these habits of obedience exerts a pressure on our will. We can evade it, but then we are attracted towards it, drawn back to it, like a pendulum which has swung away from the vertical. A certain order of things has been upset, it *must* be restored. In a word, as with all habits, we feel a sense of obligation.[27]

In some circles, the source of this "sense of obligation" is said to be the "voice" of God. Sometimes it is described as the "image of God in man." In other circles, it is described as the claims of society which the individual has "internalized." It is the "voice" of society or community that he "hears." It is the image of society reflecting in him as he gradually becomes a social being in fact rather than in potentiality alone. This growing sensitivity to the claims, regulations, and structures of the community is said to come about through a long and involved "socialization process." This socialization process is an anthropological, sociological, and psychosocial translation of the conversion or the new birth process. But what we wish to stress in this connection is that social scientists will enrich and deepen their understanding of the socialization process if they understand and study the *religious* dimension of the process. By "religious" is meant the dimension of the process that is conditioned by the sense of finitude and helplessness.

Theologians insist that morality is not simply a finite individual's invention; rather it transcends his finite wisdom. Durkheim and more recent students of religious behavior and religious institutions could not agree more, although they would add that it is the society and culture that transcend the finite individual, with morality as a facet of society and culture. Society, culture, and the physical world of nature—these are the transcendent trinity on which the finite individual depends for his very being as a person. Theologian Friedrich Schleiermacher posited that religion is the feeling or sense of one's *absolute dependence*. Each human person is absolutely dependent on society, culture, and nature. Without *nature*, he would not be even a breathing organism blessed with blood and

---

[27]Henri Bergson, *The Two Sources of Morality and Religion*, trans. R. A. Audra and C. Brereton (Garden City, N. Y.: Doubleday Anchor Books, 1956), p. 10.

interacting cells. Without *society* he would have no social interaction, no language, no companionship in his wanderings. In short, without society he would be only half created.

Without *culture*, the finite individual and his society would be at best a band of primates fumbling aimlessly and more helpless than any of the other primates, whose instinctual endowment does at least give them some direction. Culture is the structure of meaning in which human beings live and societies endure. Without it, human beings would be only potential persons and the most pitiable of animals. The human organism becomes a person only within the social womb. And the social womb without culture does not even exist except at the most meager and trivial level.

Born Again—Mystical or Practical?

Some of our readers may ask, "What does all this talk of society and culture have to do with being born again?" Our answer is that being born again *is* the process of being immersed into a new cultural framework and becoming united with a new subsociety. Paul the Apostle admonished his readers to "put on the Lord Jesus Christ" (Romans 13:14 RSV). To the church at Galatia he wrote, "For as many of you as were baptized into Christ have put on Christ" (Galatians 3:27 RSV).

When translated into psychosocial language, to "put on Christ" means something entirely practical and not mystical. It is a radical change in behavior, attitude and thought. Very concretely, it usually means exchanging some old friends for new ones. A careful reading of Paul's letters reveals vividly that his own religious conversion included finding new associates who would support him in his new way of life. This new way of life was itself an essential part of the new birth. This new way is, again, not something mystical or mysterious but something quite practical. It is a new way of talking, thinking, and behaving.

More precisely, the individual who makes a radical religious conversion will find that his *vocabulary* has undergone some serious and drastic changes. If a very meticulous social scientist so desired and could receive permission to do so, he could actually keep a detailed *record* of the number of times certain key words are used by a new charismatic convert, words which rarely appeared in his conversation before his conversion began. For example, the social scientist would note a drastic increase in the use of the phrase "the Lord Jesus Christ." Other such phrases would also be found much more frequently—for example, "Holy Spirit," "prayer," "Bible," "church," "God," "faith," "witness," "the Lord," "grace," and "Amen." If the new convert were converted to a certain kind of Christian group, he would be found using much more frequently than he had previously such words as "Satan," "demons," "angels," "tongues," "healing," "praise God," "hell," and "sinner."

It could be objected that these are mere words and that words are not the heart of a genuine religious conversion. On the contrary, while key words and phrases are not the *whole* of conversion, they are an *essential part* of the whole cloth. In addition, accompanying the change in vocabulary will be certain drastic changes in *behavior.* Instead of sleeping late on Sunday morning as he always had done, a new charismatic would be found going to church. He might also be found handing out tracts or giving his "witness" to "sinners."

Of course, there are *degrees* of conversion-behavior. Some new converts may change their behavior only to a moderate degree. However, if the behavioral changes are only slight, the convert's new friends (that is, his church) might inform him that his conversion was not genuine or that it lacked "depth" or that it was not "strong." Soon we will raise the interesting question of how *sincere* belief is determined.

Speaking psychologically and socially, being born again includes significant changes not only in vocabulary, conversation and overt behavior, but also in *thinking.* Even though we ordinarily determine what a person is thinking by what he says (and writes) and what he does, it is nevertheless important to add this change of thinking as a part of the new birth. It would be superficial indeed to count *only* the change in vocabulary and not the thinking, although to ignore this change of vocabulary would be equally superficial if the new birth is to be understood profoundly.

Some of the change in a convert's thinking can sometimes be detected in the questions he asks, as well as the questions he is reluctant to ask. A young woman who had left the Reverend Moon's Unification Church charged that this Church discouraged certain kinds of probing questions from being asked. Those who raised such questions were judged by the Unification Church leaders to be not yet "fully converted." Their thinking was not yet in harmony with the Church.

In addition, the individual's new conversion entails *positively asking certain kinds of questions* that he or she had never asked before. Such questions would be, "How can I learn more about the Reverend Moon's teachings about God?" "How can I cease thinking about my parents and, instead, focus on my work here at the center?" "What must I do in order to be more spiritual and a better servant of God and the Unification Church?" But someone who had been converted *away from* the Unification Church would ask, not these questions, but rather questions appropriate to the particular group or community to which he had been converted.

The point is that, from a psychological and social perspective, the conversion experience and transformation is not a mysterious phenomenon or work. Rather it is a number of phenomena sewn together into a pattern. These phenomena of the new birth are new thinking, new behavior, and a new language. Parents have often complained that they could not understand the language of their teenagers. Each new subculture tends to develop a language of its own. Charles Colson's Catholic wife was frightened by the strange language that her husband and his evangelical friends were using to discuss their religion. Indeed, she expressed to him another fear: "I'm just not sure how I fit into this new life of yours."[28] The new language, the behavior patterns, and new scheme of thought were all a bit disorienting to her. In addition, there were her husband's strange new friends. Colson spoke of "a whole new set of people I was meeting."[29] In our judgment, these new phenomena were not mere symptoms of Colson's new birth. They *were and are* the major ingredients of his new birth.

"Do I Really Believe?"

Luke Maple (as we will call him) walked with one of us through the neighborhood one afternoon and talked about his religious faith. He had studied to be a Roman Catholic priest but had decided not to continue on this track. But he still regarded himself as a faithful Roman Catholic. At the same time, he had spent many months in profound anxiety about whether he *really* believed. Here is some of the conversation:

Luke. I have looked deep into my mind and heart to see whether I have faith, whether I really have true belief.

Joe. What did you find?

Luke. Well, sometimes I have prayed and found God. There were times when I seemed really to know God as the heavenly Father.

Joe. At other times?

Luke. At other times—nothing. I just don't know whether I have genuine faith or not. Half the time I feel I don't. I want to, but I don't.

Joe. You think of faith or belief as a stirring inside your body?

Luke. In a sense—in my mind or heart, anyhow. There ought to be some feeling, something there that you just know is faith or genuine belief. Sometimes I believe, sometimes I don't. I'm ambivalent. Maybe I only half believe. But how can you have half a belief?

Joe. Maybe there's another way to look at it.

Luke. What do you mean?

---

[28]Charles Colson, *Born Again*, p. 177.

[29]Ibid., p. 210.

Joe. Let me ask you: Do you use the rosary regularly?

Luke. No, I don't use it any more at all.

Joe. Do you go to confession?

Luke. Not very often—some.

Joe. Do you go to mass regularly, faithfully?

Luke. About half the time.

Joe. Do you pray regularly?

Luke. Well, we pray at meals and I pray with the kids and my wife at night.

Joe. Do you pray often alone, or maybe with just your wife?

Luke. Well, Joe, mostly I worry and read a lot. I don't pray as much as I used to.

Joe. I suspect, Luke, that you will never be able to regard yourself as having genuine or true faith in God until your *behavior* changes.

Luke. What behavior?

Joe. Well, as I see it, you are ambivalent about whether you have faith because your behavior is ambivalent. I mean, you think you have half faith because your behavior is actually about half (or less) of what you grew up to expect from a faithful Christian. You don't pray regularly, go to church regularly, or do other so-called religious behaviors regularly. So, it isn't surprising to find that you aren't sure that you have Christian faith. Your faith *is* your behavior, or at least a major part of it.

The conversation continued. Luke had already acknowledged that he did not always *think* the way the very faithful Catholic was, in Luke's mind, supposed to think. Indeed, he had raised some very severe and penetrating questions and could not answer them firmly or in the way that he grew up expecting a strong Christian to answer them. What Luke had to face was this: On the one hand, he could openly acknowledge that his "belief" or "faith" was not some mysterious essence inside the mind or heart (but rather was a whole complex of special behavior, thinking, and language). Or, on the other hand, he could continue searching fruitlessly for the mysterious inner essence. If he should take the first alternative, he would then be faced with a choice: either (1) recognize that he was neither practicing nor thinking strongly in accord with his definition of what a Christian is, or (2) redefine what "being a Christian believer" means, that is, redefine it in such a way as to introduce new kinds of thinking and behavior.

Some people define 'Christian' in terms of "ultimate concern." And the ultimate concern could be identified overtly as wrestling with the kind of questions that plagued Luke. There are many groups who attempt to define what Christianity *really* is. A careful study shows that these groups vary considerably (in the thinking, behavior, and language) on what they designate as "Christian faith." It is not our purpose here to lay down what Christianity really is. But we do wish to stress that no religion can get off the ground without marking off a certain content of *thinking* as uniquely its own. In earlier chapters we stressed the essential role of metaphysical and philosophical beliefs in religion.

In the next chapter we will deal with this important subject of religious metaphysics. We will begin with the revolutionary metaphysical position of the Apostle Paul. His conversion cannot be profoundly understood or appreciated without some basic grasp of his philosophical framework. It is a part of the early Christian "culture," which gave "meaning" to the social behavior and the psychological response of the early Christians.

Chapter VI

The Theological and Philosophical Dimensions of the New Birth

The Crucial Question

There is a question that must be faced but which we have postponed facing until now. It can be formulated in a number of ways, but we will formulate it so that most of our readers will immediately recognize it to be a crucial question of far-reaching implications. It is this: "Suppose reality is not what evangelical Christians say it is, then is their own new birth experience simply a delusion?" Almost all evangelicals would say that the Mormon's new birth experience is a delusion. We have discussed the following issue with evangelicals: "People appear to have been converted through all sorts of religions, so that their lives have been changed significantly. There are many Black Muslim believers today who can testify to the radical change that came into their lives through their conversion. For example, drug addicts, robbers, extortionists, murderers, rapists, and a variety of criminals and law-breakers have been transformed into law-abiding citizens since becoming Black Muslims. Are their conversions simply delusions? Or do they prove that Allah is really God and that he is at work in the lives of millions of people today?"

The responses that evangelicals have given to these above statements and questions vary somewhat. At one end of the line is the blunt reply that Satan tries to simulate everything that Christ does in order to divert people from the true faith. The Black Muslims, then, are regarded as simply the tools of a very clever plan that Satan has put into action.

In a southern city of the United States is an Assembly of God minister—we will call him Raymond Magee—who as a young man was a pimp for prostitutes. His father was an alcoholic and very poor. Raymond had engaged in a variety of unlawful acts and regarded himself as an outcast from decent society. Fortunately, a group of "church folks" in the rural area where Raymond grew up managed to persuade him to come to their little church for a revival meeting. While at the meeting, the following happened: Raymond suddenly "fell under conviction" and found himself praying for forgiveness. In the process of this experience, he began shouting and expressing himself with great enthusiasm. To the surprise of those rejoicing aloud with him, Raymond in his exuberance embraced a hot pot-belly stove. To the astonishment of all, he seemed not to be burned or pained by the experience. That happened in 1946. In 1975 the one of us who had known Raymond for over twenty years listened to him relate this experience and explain how it had not only changed his life, but rendered all doubts about his theology inconsequential.

In the course of the conversation, Raymond was told that in India and in other parts of the world, some individuals have had experiences of successfully resisting both hot objects and sharp instruments. Many of these individuals regarded their extraordinary experience as the obvious manifestation of the power and truth of their religion. To this, Raymond had a ready answer: "True, those extraordinary experiences did actually take place, but they were the workings of Satan in his desire to deceive the very elect of God if possible." The Reverend Raymond Magee was, however, ready to defend his own experience against those Christians who believe that the Charismatic movement as well as the earlier Holiness and Pentecostal movements are all themselves works of Satan.

A Problem of Theology

Bewildered by the charges and counter-charges that many Christians (and others) hurl at the beliefs of one another, some religious believers have come up with the following alternative: Why not regard the conversions of Mormons, Muslims, Black Muslims, Buddhists, Baptists, charismatic Episcopalians, Methodists, and Hare Krishnas as *all* genuine conversions?

The interesting thing is that most of those Baptists, charismatic Episcopalians, Mormons, Muslims, and others who take their own conversions quite seriously cannot in good faith take seriously the conversion-claims of others. Mormons honestly think that their conversions are genuine and that the Buddhists' conversions are not. Indeed, Theravadan Buddhists do not believe in God. But do the Mormons believe in God? Evangelical or orthodox Christians reply that the Mormon God can by no stretch of the imagination be identified with the true God. In short, the Mormons are told that they only *think* that their God does in fact exist. It is very interesting that Dr. Charles Hartshorne and Dr. Alvin Plantinga—two of the leading contemporary proponents of the ontological argument for the existence of God—have been slow to recognize that *they are not even talking about the same God*. Each thinks that the ontological argument proves the existence of God, but neither could with consistency recognize the other's concept of God to be legitimate. If Dr. Hartshorne's concept of God is accepted, then Plantinga's must be rejected as morally inferior, so much so that Plantinga's alleged God is unworthy of that sacred name.

Levels of Genuineness

Could a Mormon consistently hold that the Black Muslim converts are not genuinely converted? Could Billy Graham consistently hold that an evangelical Christian who converts to the Mormon faith has not had a genuine conversion? Indeed, what constitutes an authentic new birth? How is it to be distinguished from a counterfeit new birth? A naturalist holds that there is no God. Which raises the question as to whether he could consistently believe that Billy Graham, Mormons, Black Muslims, Presbyterians, or anyone has in reality been born again.

We suggest that while these questions cannot be easily answered, they can be broken down into more manageable parts. A naturalist can surely observe the significant changes in the lives of some of the converts of Billy Graham's crusades. Even though he does not believe there is a God, the naturalist can with consistency recognize that there is some connection between an individual's giving up a life of crime and his joining the Black Muslims, the Baptists, the Mormons or some other religious body. By the same token, the Mormons ought to be able to observe when a person's hostility toward others is replaced by general friendly behavior toward others when he joins the Unitarian Church or becomes a serious student of religious humanism.

The three levels of conversion or being born again that we discuss in this book are: (1) the social level, (2) the psychological level, and (3) the metaphysical, cultural, or philosophical level. The question of whether a person's alleged conversion is *genuine* simply cannot be answered until we know which one of these levels is under consideration.

It is at the metaphysical level that we find most disagreements. We will explain why. Consider the car thief who was converted in a Southern Baptist revival meeting. A Muslim could normally agree that at the *social* level the conversion is genuine. That is, his behavior has changed. Richard Nixon's former hatchet man Charles W. Colson claims to have had a "spiritual rebirth." This will be disputed by various groups because the word "spiritual" often entails certain metaphysical beliefs. Be that as it may, Colson's *social* behavior has changed significantly. He is no longer involved in crimes. So his conversion will be regarded by many people to be genuine at the social level even though they may have serious doubts about the other two levels.

Of course, if there is no supernatural Christ or theological superstructure of the kind which evangelical Christians speak of, then Colson's conversion is not genuine at the *metaphysical or philosophical* level. As an evangelical Christian, Colson flatly denies that the conversions to non-Christian religions are genuine at this metaphysical level. But this need not entail a denial of their genuineness at the *social* level.

The *psychological* level of conversion is more difficult than the social level to discuss coherently. This is because the psychological aspect is very private. The language that we use in public is not very precise in revealing private responses. Nevertheless, it is possible to say that a person may personally *feel* his life to be meaningful and enjoyable. He may *experience* contentment and peace. He may even *want* to be kind and considerate, whereas before his conversion he did not. Indeed, these changes in his feelings, subjective experiences, wants, and desires *are his conversion or new birth at the psychological level.*

A person's psychological states may *really exist* even when his beliefs are in serious error. Evangelical Christians will acknowledge that a Mormon can *feel* that he is in favor with God and can *experience* peace psychologically in believing that he will not go to hell. But, according to the evangelical Christian position, while the Mormon's mental states may be *genuine as psychological conditions,* they will not be based on a solid and *genuine theological foundation.* The Mormon can go to hell even though psychologically he may be experiencing euphoria.

Can a person really be born again? Considerable agreement could be found to the effect that a person can genuinely be born again at both the social level and the psychological level. The hard debate comes at the metaphysical or theological level, for it is here that profound and severe disagreements come into play.* In the remainder of this chapter we will be

---

*Speaking to a group of students at the evangelical Wheaton College, Billy Graham announced in 1980 that he would give up using the phrase *born again*, in favor of *born from above* (which is an alternate reading given in the ASV and RSV of John 3:3,7). The phrase *born from above* emphasizes Graham's conviction that the new birth is a supernatural divine work.

dealing with only a few—although important—aspects of the problem of the metaphysical genuineness of the new birth.

Revolution in Science and Religion

Most of the writers of the New Testament believed that their Christianity had deep roots in the Hebrew faith and tradition. Christianity could not have developed out of the ancient Chinese tradition of Confucianism. Nor could Confucianism have developed out of the Hebrew tradition. A belief system as rich and complex as that of, say, the Apostle Paul or the author of the Book of Hebrews does not come about by mere spontaneous generation. Early Christianity had deep roots; and, as New Testament scholars have shown, it had also *many* roots, only one of which was the Hebrew faith. It is quite unlikely that the Christian belief-system could have come about without roots in both the Hebrew culture and the Hellenistic culture, just as Einstein's theory of relativity would not likely have developed independent of its roots in the long history of Western physics, mathematics, astronomy, and philosophy.

There is something which science and religion have in common. Each has a long and fascinating intellectual tradition out of which its present state has grown. By understanding better their own intellectual heritage, both science and religion gain insight into and appreciation of their current positions.

It is sometimes said that science has one way of thinking, whereas religion has another. This view is very misleading. Religion and science may have different goals, problems and motivations, but each engages in the same thinking process when thinking is going on. This does not mean that science and religion do not sometimes come into conflict regarding certain theories and views. This is to be expected. After all, physicists sometimes disagree with one another on critical issues, as do the spokesmen of the various religions.

Indeed, as Thomas Kuhn has shown, there have been significant periods in the history of science when it has slowly but surely created its own great revolutions.[1] Similarly, a religious tradition will sometimes produce a great religious revolution. Christianity was a part of one such revolution in the first century. In a very real sense, a religion can go through a sweeping and profound conversion of its own, and the people who happen to be living in the tradition at that time may find themselves going through a transformation by reflecting in their own lives the conversion or

---

[1]See Thomas Kuhn, *The Structure of Scientific Revolutions*, 2nd ed. rev. (Chicago: University of Chicago Press, 1970), chapters 9-13.

revolution taking place in their religious tradition. Saul of Tarsus (later known as Paul the Apostle) was one such person. His Pharisaic Judaism underwent a revolution in which he became not only personally caught up, but also a leading spokesman. The words "free" and "freedom" occur throughout his epistles, for they are the watchwords of a major personality of a genuine religious revolution. Let us now look into the conflict that was taking place in Paul's life and mind, a conflict that eventually demanded a resolution. In Paul's life the resolution came as a dramatic and powerful *theological, metaphysical,* or *cultural* breakthrough.

The Development of Contradictions in the Hebrew Tradition

The Hebrew religion of Paul's time was not simply the psychological states of Jewish believers. It was in addition an objective network of theological and metaphysical doctrines and teachings. By the time early Christianity began to appear on the scene, the Hebrew Bible had already been translated into Greek and had already become a central part of Hebrew culture throughout much of the Roman Empire. Paul inherited this culture as a part of his own intellectual and moral environment. He was also born into a world in which the Hellenistic culture, with its many strands, came up against the ancient Hebrew culture, with its many strands. Paul's own life was a stage upon which these two mighty cultures encountered each other.

Philosophers of science have shown that often progress is made when a scientific tradition uncovers contradictions in its own theories and claims.[2] By detecting its own contradictions, a science offers itself the opportunity to produce better explanations. A very similar procedure can be seen at work in the history of theology.[3] This does not mean that either science or theology has a guarantee that by uncovering some of its deepest contradictions it will develop a better system. Rather, the door of opportunity for improvement is often opened to the tradition that can critically analyze its own theories and beliefs.

Before plunging into the theological journey of the Apostle Paul, we will pause to deal briefly with the objection sometimes raised that religion does not need metaphysics and that metaphysics is even a hindrance to it. Our response is that *every* religion has its own peculiar metaphysics. This

---

[2]See Imre Lakatos and Alan Musgrave, eds., *Criticism and the Growth of Knowledge: Proceedings of the International Colloquium in the Philosophy of Science, London, 1965,* vol. 4 (New York: Cambridge University Press, 1970).

[3]See J. E. Barnhart, *The Study of Religion and Its Meaning* (New York: Walter de Gruyter, Inc., 1977), chapters 9 and 11.

is simply because believers make all sorts of statements and claims to truth. A person cannot belive *in* something unless he believes at least implicitly *that* such and such is truly the case about this something he believes in. If a Buddhist claims that he merely gives witness to his religious experience, he will in the very process of witnessing utter all kinds of metaphysical and theological statements which Christians, Muslims, and Jews will find questionable at the very least. The Apostle Paul was quite aware of making numerous theological assertions when he wrote his letters. But one reason that some religious believers wish to deny that they make theological claims is that they seem to want to avoid any possibility of having anyone detect contradiction in their claims.

Applying the Belief-System

It is important to see how contradictions in the metaphysical or theological system tend to come about in the first place. The most obvious explanation is that religious believers attempt to *apply* their theological beliefs to many areas of everyday life. But in doing this, they have to increase the *number of statements or claims* about how their religion will apply to this and that area of life. As the number of such statements are increased, the greater is the risk that some of these statements will come into contradiction with each other. This is especially true the more exact and definite the claims become, as can be observed in any vital system of beliefs, whether theology, astronomy, or physics.

Extending the Belief-System

There is a second way in which theology—or any belief-system—runs the risk of developing inconsistencies. It is the way of *extension*. A vital and dynamic belief-system tends to extend its territory or domain. As we pointed out in an earlier chapter, the Apostle Paul's theology expanded to the point of including statements not only about God, but also about the psychological make-up of human beings. Furthermore, Paul's theology moved into such realms as morality, marriage, cosmology, politics, and local customs. He both applied and expanded his theological explanation of things.

A good explanation is designed to cover a lot of territory. In doing so, it also increases the chances of running into trouble. But it would be self-defeating to reduce the scope of an explanation to the point that its claims become obvious but trivial. Granted, a timid and shallow explanation, by not venturing out, may avoid running into self-contradiction. But it would then explain very little. We wish, therefore, to emphasize that a theological system that develops serious contradictions may be more fruitful than a system of thought that says very little or has no practical application. A risky theological system can sometimes contribute to the growth of knowledge and metaphysics, provided its contradictions are noted, seriously attended to, and wrestled with. Paul certainly detected contradictions in his Hebrew theology, and he wrestled with them profoundly. His Christian theology was a bold and daring attempt to come up with a more powerful and coherent system than he had inherited. Turning now to look at Paul's *theological* pilgrimage, we can see how he strove courageously both to apply and to extend what he believed in as a devout Pharisee.

The Jewish Culture Confronting the Hellenistic Culture

It is important to know that before his conversion, Paul was a loyal member of the Jewish school of the Pharisees rather than the Sadducees. This is important because the Pharisees were the Jewish leaders who not only were well trained in the Jewish law, but actively engaged in attempting to *apply* their faith to the problems they encountered daily in the Hellenistic world. The Sadducees did not try to deal extensively with the Mediterranean culture that the Greeks, Romans, and even the Persians had helped to develop. The Hellenistic and Mediterranean culture in Paul's time was riddled with doctrines about personal resurrection, angels, saviors, demons, salvation, cosmic battles, and cosmic deliverance. While the Sadducees tended to ignore these doctrines, they had no explanation as to why belief in such doctrines was so widespread. By contrast, the Pharisees attempted to *extend* their theology to cover these doctrines. Indeed, they went so far as to agree with their pagan neighbors that there actually did exist cosmic spirits, demons, angels, and personal resurrection. Paul grew up in this Pharisaic tradition with its extended and searching theology.

The noted archeologist and Biblical scholar W. F. Albright noted that the major differences between the Sadducees and the Pharisees

> were basically due to the different ways in which Jewish groups reacted to the challenge of the Hellenistic way of thinking....In spite of the fact that it was the Sadducees who first came under strong Hellenistic influence . . ., it was the Pharisees who eventually became more thoroughly Hellenized. In fact we are hardly going too far to say that the Pharisaic movement represents the Hellenization of the normative Jewish position. . . . All this emphasis [by the Pharisees] on the value of systematic study [of the law] and on the *widest possible scope* of education was foreign to early Israel.... Pharisaic insistence on the need of *extending* the operation of the Law to suit new

conditions and to cover all possible eventualities was thoroughly Hellenistic.[4]

But Paul believed that some critical problems had developed in his expanding Pharasaic theology. He detected cracks in the dam. Questioning whether the Torah (the Hebrew Law of God) was sufficient to deal effectively with demons, Satan, pervasive guilt, cosmic spirits and death, Paul eventually concluded that the Law could not deal with them. This meant to him that his inherited faith was in the throes of a severe and major crisis. The Hebrew Law had developed over the centuries as a way of dealing with very practical and earthly applications of the faith of Israel. But like so many who had been influenced by the Hellenistic culture of his time, Paul thought that there actually were not only earthly powers and conflicts, but *cosmic* powers, cosmic spirits, and cosmic conflicts with which mortal men and women had to contend. He came to believe that the Law had little to say regarding these cosmic matters and problems. For Paul, the Law had nothing compelling to say about how to cope with demons, death, countless celestial beings, and a pervasive sense of guilt.

Ancient Jewish theology had promised that if the Law were properly observed, the faithful would enjoy favor and peace with God. But as a strict and faithful Pharisee, Paul became convinced that the cosmic demons and principalities, as well as his guilt, were destroying his peace with God. They were, in effect, coming between God and man, and the Law seemed to Paul to be powerless to deal with this unparalleled crisis. Something somewhere had to give!

The Pressure on Pharisaic Judaism

Had he not been thoroughly versed in his Pharisaic theological tradition, Paul could not have felt so keenly the contradictions that had arisen within it. Had he not been a careful thinker, he likely would not have attempted to *deduce* from his theological premises their logical conclusions. And had he not looked courageously at these conclusions, he might not have detected what seemed to him to be inconsistencies among them. It was the pressure of being aware of these inconsistencies that forced Paul's mind into unconscious and creative depths. He personally suffered the internal conflicts of his Pharisaic theological system because he took it seriously and tried to live by it. Later he would write of himself, "I advanced in Judaism beyond many of my own age" (Galatians 1:14 RSV). He was wholly committed to live his life by the promises, premises, claims, theories, and

---

[4]W. F. Albright, *From the Stone Age to Christianity*, 2nd ed. (Garden City, N.Y.: Anchor Books, Doubleday, 1957), pp. 354-55. Italics and words in brackets are added.

directions that his own Rabbinic tradition had formulated over the years regarding such matters as sin, salvation, death, elemental spirits, demons, Satan, angels, the centrality of the Law, and peace and favor with God.

Indeed, his Pharisaic tradition had begun to *expand* the canon of the Scripture—adding the Prophets (200 B.C.) and later the Writings (90 A.D.) to the Torah (Law). In addition, Pharisaism developed new ritual practices, such as hallowing the paschal meal and the baptism of proselytes. These last two in particular seem to have been responses to the rituals of certain rival religions of the Hellenistic world. Indeed, in Paul's letters he spoke also of union with God, which was a major theme of various mystery religions of the first century A.D. The ancient faith of Israel had no concept of any metaphysical "union" between God and his followers. It was a concept that grew up in the wider Mediterranean world and may even have been transported from further east of Palestine.

The Essenes and various religions of the Hellenistic world—including the mystery religions—were already practicing both baptism and the sacred meal before Christianity appeared. But perhaps more important for the rise of Christianity, these religions were also making fantastic claims about what their rituals could effect. The effects were said to be universal and cosmic in *scope*. If the proselyting Pharisees were to compete, they had to counter with their own special claims and explanations regarding the power of their sacred meal and their baptism of new converts. But to make sweeping claims and promises is to run the risk of having them checked and tested. Our view is that Paul's own personal life was a kind of laboratory experiment in which some of these new directions in Pharisaic theology were being tested out.

The New Cosmic Expectations

The Pharisaic Judaism that nourished Paul in the first century of our era gave clear signs of a steady movement in two directions, the *cosmic* direction and the *individualistic* direction. Unlike the Sadducees of the first century, the Pharisees believed that salvation had more than an earthly fulfillment. Salvation had a cosmic sweep, embodying a Cosmic Drama in which each individual's life had a very special and everlasting role. The Law (Torah), too, had a special role—as the primary link between heaven and earth, between spirit and flesh. Pharisaic Judaism perceived the Law as the ladder on which the faithful could ascend to favor with God.

In China during the Han dynasty, which was roughly at the time of the rise of the Pharisaic movement in Israel, the Chinese Emperor was viewed as the *personal* link between heaven and earth. It was he who personally performed the primary rituals and effected peace between the order of heaven and the affairs of human mortals. It was he who, above all others, represented the people to heaven, and, in turn, represented heaven to the people. To be sure, the ritual, the ceremony, and the procedures by which the Emperor carried out his mediating function were all carried out according to rule or law. In his role as mediator, the Emperor was revered as a person, a more-than-human person, providing a power and vitality that the impersonal law was unable to provide.

Paul believed that the Law of his Pharisaic faith was without power and vitality. For him, the Law existed as only a reminder of both the divine standards and the human failure to live up to the standards. Unlike the Chinese Emperor, the Law could not *effect* anything. It could neither *present* man to God nor *represent* man's case to God in the way that the mystery religions of Paul's time claimed to be able to do (or the way the Chinese Emperor was believed to be able to do). Paul's experience with the Law of his Pharisaic heritage had left him with a sense of its failure to measure up to his new religious expectations. For him, the Law was lacking in two crucial and critical areas.

First, it did not serve as a ladder on which the individual could ascend with certainty to God. The Law was more like a mirror revealing to him his sinfulness. Second, the Law was abstract, not personal and not cosmic. It was not the deity himself personally involved in human life and in cosmic conflict. Paul came to feel a critical need for some infinitely powerful Being who, through direct encounter with death and mortal finitude, would somehow triumph over all earthly and cosmic enemies of human flesh (that is, over all human finitude). The abstract Law simply was unable to fulfill Paul's rising expectations. Clearly, both Paul's general theological orientation and the new demands that he had begun to make on his theology combined to generate a crisis and need for a theological breakthrough. And that is precisely where Paul's theory of the *cosmic Lord Jesus Christ* came into the picture. This Cosmic Being was projected as the perfect metaphysical means for doing what the impersonal Law could not do.

Early Christian theology as expressed in Paul's epistles, in the Book of Hebrews, and in certain other first century writings was a theological revolution to replace the old order, the old metaphysical "map." It was the new covenant, the new testament. Indeed, some of Paul's letters and the Book of Hebrews went even further than the Chinese religion, which had not demanded that the Emperor-Mediator be sinless and perfect. Paul and the author of Hebrews required their Cosmic Mediator to be perfect in every way, since, they believed, human sin was infinite and since the power of the demonic host was cosmic in outreach.

We believe that it is absolutely imperative to see that this metaphysical revolution was not one of pure theory (that is, theology alone). It was also a revolution at the moral and emotional levels. It is, nevertheless, possible to focus on the metaphysical or theological level exclusively and to study it as if it were an independent cultural process of its own. This would be like studying the development of, say, the English language over a period of 300 years without reference to the emotions and morals of those who spoke the language. All important studies lay aside certain aspects of life temporarily in order to concentrate more thoroughly on other aspects. In this chapter, we must focus on the theological process, but we do not forget that theology was a vital part of the personal lives of Paul and other Jews, Hellenists, and Christians of the first century.

The New Birth of the Entire Universe

Although early Israelite faith had no place for the individual's resurrection from death, the mystery religions of the Mediterranean world of Paul's time were built around a savior-god who had died and been resurrected. Through this unparalleled cosmic event, the victorious savior-god was believed to have secured salvation and the guarantee of resurrection for his individual devotees. Many of the Jews had for centuries enjoyed hopes of a Messiah (anointed Leader) who would grow up in their midst and lead them to their destiny as the People of God *on earth*. But by the time Paul was born, this sort of Messianic hope had suffered severe setbacks (contradictions and falsifications). The situation was so critical that many Jews—including some of the most respected Pharisees—were turning to an other-worldly vision. Like their neighbors of the pagan mystery religions, many Jews began to look for a *cosmic* deliverance rather than one that would somehow develop on earth. Some heavenly, celestial Being with cosmic power was required to bring forth a complete and cataclysmic transformation of the most drastic and sweeping scope imaginable. The whole universe—nature included—would be converted, born again!

Some writers have claimed that early Christianity did not emphasize a change in the environment or in external circumstance, but instead focused entirely on an "inward change of heart." But they are in error in this claim. First century Christians shared with many of their neighbors in the trend to expect the entire environment and all external circumstance to undergo a complete and total transformation. In the Epistle to the Romans, Paul says that the entire universe is awaiting its own redemption and conversion (see Romans 8:19-23). The author of II Peter speaks of the day when "the heavens will be kindled and dissolved, and the elements will melt with fire! But . . . we wait for new heavens and a new earth in which righteousness dwells" (II Peter 3:12-13 RSV).

In his book *Roots of Renewal in Myth and Madness: The Meaning of Psychotic Episodes,* John W. Perry insists that at the heart of the creative symbolic process in acute psychotic episodes are such "common phenomena as the death and rebirth fantasies or world destruction and recreation fantasies." Indeed, he goes on to write that in times of cultural change, prophets are in effect, through their visions, experimenting with new values and meanings. Sometimes cultural changes and the prophetic probings "make their appearance in visionary states that closely resemble psychotic episodes."[5] Today, when especially in the United States all sorts of religious cults and traditions seem to be projecting weird and exotic myths, their critics would do well to look for possible signs of creative probings in the midst of the putative psychosis behind the metaphysical projections.

To say that a vision is an element of a psychotic episode is not to say that it is therefore a vision without reality and substance. It may plug into objective reality or it may not. Like any metaphysical belief, it needs to be examined, debated, and tested in whatever ways can be found for testing. If Paul's metaphysical belief system proves to be unwarranted in our day, it will not be because it was born of Paul's own psychotic episode. Therefore, in suggesting that Paul's revolutionary theology was evoked by a psychotic episode, we do not wish this suggestion in itself to be given excessive weight. Our point is that Paul's own psychosis was largely a microcosm or reflection of the two cultures—the Jewish and the Hellenistic—coming together as two powerful fronts to produce severe psychological turbulence and eventually a creative theological breakthrough. ("Psychosis" is not to be thought of as a disease.)

This is to imply, not that early Christianity produced the final and authoritative metaphysical framework, but rather that, given the presuppositions of Pharisaic Judaism of Paul's time, Christianity produced some resolutions to problems spawned by those presuppositions. It eliminated certain serious contradictions and developed a more flexible model than Pharisaic theology alone was able to do. It may be that certain of the key presuppositions that both Pharisaic and Christian theology held in common should be discarded, but that is another issue. We turn to look now at the early Christian "resolution," which Christians like Paul regarded to be a transformation and fulfillment of his Rabbinic belief system. We will see how Paul took the old metaphysical "map" and reshaped it into a new one.

---

[5](San Francisco: Jossey-Bass Publishers, 1976), pp. 8-9.

The Christian Son of God

As a monotheistic Jew, Paul could not easily embrace the pagan idea of a savior-god, but there was clearly the need for such a savior-god to deal with the kinds of critical problems that had developed *within the Hellenistic popular culture.* If Paul could not even imagine that the God of Israel had died and been resurrected, neither could he see any point in claiming that a mere angel had died and been resurrected. An angel, like creaturely human beings, could not successfully wage cosmic battle and gain everlasting victories in the way that the savior-god of the mystery religions was said to be able to do. *Clearly, Paul's Rabbinic Judaism needed a cosmic and divine figure to compete with the bold claims of the pagan savior-god.*

Paul came to envision "the Son of God," who could be divine—reflecting the fullness of God—without being God in the strict sense of the term. It would be outrageous blasphemy for a Jew to claim that God had died and been resurrected. But a Jew might be able to make this claim about the *Son* of God. To be sure, this concept of the Son of God was vague at certain crucial points, and that is what gave it a strategic advantage. Its vagueness rendered it flexible and fruitful, at least up to a point.

Although never clearly referring to his dying savior-god as "God" (*theos*), Paul does call him "Lord" (*kurios*). This flexible word *kurios* sometimes means "Sir." But it also can be used to mean "Lord" (in the sense of divinity) and is actually used in the Greek version of the Old Testament to translate the Hebrew word *Yahweh*, which is the sacred name that God was thought to have revealed to Moses. By using this word *kurios* to refer to his savior-god, Paul gives him the authority and power of divinity without straightforwardly calling him God.

In various epistles, Paul refers to this savior-god as "the Lord Jesus Christ" (see Romans 1:1, 7; 5:1; 7:25; I Corinthians 1:2; II Corinthians 1:3; Galatians 1:3; 6:14, 18; Philippians 1:2; 4:23; etc.). The word "Christ" (*Christos*) is the Greek equivalent of the Hebrew Messiah. In the Greek, *Iesous* designates Jesus or Joshua (which in Hebrew means "deliverance" or "salvation" [Ieshovah]). Jesus (Greek) or Joshua (Hebrew) is an abbreviated form of the Hebrew name *Jehoshua*, which means "Yahweh is Salvation." Professor G.A. Wells, in *The Jesus of the Early Christians*, shows that at least one of the many self-proclaimed Messiahs in the first century A.D. in Palestine purported to be another Joshua who would lead his followers dry-shod across the Jordan.[6] Indeed,

---

[6]See G.A. Wells, *The Jesus of the Early Christians: A Study in Christian Origins* (Buffalo, N.Y.: Prometheus Books, 1971), pp. 4-5.

Paul himself refers to "another Jesus [*allon Iesoun*]" (II Corinthians 11:4), who perhaps was another one of the many self-proclaimed Messiahs, saviors, or deliverers so prevalent at the time.

Christ Supersedes the Law in the Theological Revolution

The paradigm shift in Paul's metaphysics and cosmology is most dramatically illustrated in the way Jesus the Messiah and Lord supersedes the Law of Pharisaic Judaism. No longer is the Law the mediator between man and God. As is often true in a paradigm shift, a central model of the old paradigm is relegated to an inferior place, if it is retained at all. One of the perpetual debates among the early Christians was the status of the Law in comparison to that of the Lord Jesus Christ. Paul states bluntly that the Law did not proceed *directly* from God but was "ordained by angels through an intermediary" (Galatians 3:19 RSV). In his cosmology, Paul retains the Law but *demotes* it. The Law does not even stand in direct comparison to the cosmic and heavenly Jesus Christ,

> who, though he was in the form of God, did not count equality with God a thing to be grasped, but emptied himself, taking the form of a servant, being born in the likeness of men. . . . Therefore God has highly exalted him and bestowed on him the name which is above every name, that at the name of Jesus every knee should bow, in heaven and on earth and under the earth, and every tongue confess that Jesus Christ is Lord, to the glory of God the Father (Philippians 2:6-11 RSV).

By contrast, the Law is now pictured as never having had a position beyond that of a custodian. "So . . . the law," Paul wrote

> was our custodian until Christ came, that we might be justified by faith [rather than by the works of the Law]. But now that faith has come, we are no longer under a custodian; for in Christ Jesus you are all sons of God, through faith (Galatians 3:24-26 RSV).[7]

The Joy of a Released Prisoner

Max Weber many years ago called attention to the theme of overpowering joy that rings throughout the writings of the Apostle Paul.[8]

---

[7]The words in brackets are ours, but they reflect Paul's thinking in especially Galatians and Romans.

[8]See Max Weber, *The Sociology of Religion*, p. 260.

It is only by seeing Paul against the background of his involved metaphysics and theology that his joy makes any sense. Imagine a woman drinking water at the office water cooler, when suddenly she laughs joyfully. Observing her, we can surmise that she is not laughing at a joke because the laughter is too engrossing, too moving. It is a laughter of pure joy. But still her laughter may make no sense to us unless we learn what is going on within her frame of reference. We learn that she has just received a phone call from her attorney telling her that she will not, after all, be forced to be tried for murder, since the real murderer has just been caught and has confessed. Now we can make sense of her joy, her sense of release, her feelings of new freedom. It is a new day, a new life for her.

Paul believed that he was a prisoner not only of his own guilt and sinfulness, but also of the Law and of oppressive demonic beings. He actually believed that he was a trapped and condemned man—a prisoner of real forces of cosmic dimension. It is difficult for many people today to step inside this metaphysical framework, but it is necessary to do so imaginatively if one wishes to understand and appreciate the absolute breathtaking power of Paul's conversion or new birth.

Paul's metaphysical vision of Christ as the deliverer and redeemer of enslaved humanity came to him when he apparently had no road open to him inside his old Rabbinic paradigm of thought. We cannot in this book go into a detailed examination of the way in which early Christianity represents an entire cultural shift that was forced to draw on past motifs and models, to reformulate them in a revolutionary way, and then to project a radically new metaphysical vision which was believed to be divinely given. It is as if people were lost in a strange land until they discover in their midst a map to guide them out of their fruitless wanderings.

In the Tradition of Paul the Apostle

It seems altogether fair to say that the genuine heirs of the great scientists are not those who today slavishly believe what those scientists once believed in centuries past. Einstein was within the spirit and tradition of the great philosophers and scientists because he sought still more light and truth and did not surrender his thinking to anyone. Indeed, Einstein would have excluded himself from the scientific tradition had he simply embraced as the final word the theories of Newton, Kepler, Thales, and the other great thinkers of the past.

By the same token, the true heirs of Paul the Apostle and other profound religious figures are not those who slavishly try to believe one of the metaphysical or theological systems of the past. Rather, the true heirs are those who, like Paul, courageously strive to live out the premises and implications of their own belief-system. If and when their belief-system develops severe problems and contradictions, those who are in the tradition of Paul will not pretend that the difficulties do not exist. Rather, they will seek to resolve them.

All profoundly religious people have in common a sense of their own finitude. How they come to terms with their finitude determines how the various religions differ and doubtless will continue to differ with one another. In this chapter we have shown how metaphysics and theology are human attempts to find a "map" that will give them direction and orientation in a world threatened by chaos. Because no human being beyond the level of early childhood can function without metaphysical beliefs, we conclude that the metaphysical dimension of religion will not— and cannot—be eliminated so long as the human species survives. When anyone's personal metaphysical "map" begins to reveal signs of self-contradiction or serious flaw, he will respond in at least one of the following ways: (1) attempt to cover up the flaw and deny it; (2) attempt to correct the flaw or revise the map; or (3) convert by following another metaphysical "map" that promises to guide him through the threat of chaos.

Metaphysical Disorientation

When a person becomes what we call "metaphysically disoriented," he is unable to locate himself or to distinguish cosmos from chaos at certain critical points. At that moment, he becomes extremely vulnerable and susceptible to conversion by those who would sweep him into their orbit without providing him the opportunity to evaluate critically what is happening to him. Today, there is much talk on television, radio, and in newspapers and magazines about the use of brainwashing tactics in bringing about a drastic and sweeping conversion in the lives of especially young men and women. In a later chapter we will discuss so-called brainwashing and other questionable tactics of religious recruitment. But we must first offer a theoretical framework that throws a positive light on conversion as a creative transformation process for the individual.

Chapter VII

The Creation of New Desires

What Dictates Our Desires?

Earlier we spoke of free choice in terms of satisfaction of the individual's desires or wants. To cause a person to do something against his desire is to override his free choice at that point. What we have carefully avoided discussing until now is the process by which an individual is induced (or simply caused) to *change his desires and wants*. Libertarians and the national officers of the American Civil Liberties Union seem to be so strong in their defense of free choice that they fail to explore how the individual's choices are brought into being in the first place. As members of the ACLU, we strongly support its legal defense of the rights of youths to adhere to the religion of their choice. But those who believe in the principles of the open society can no longer afford to ignore the tough issues revolving around the fact that no one's desires are generated in a vacuum. Many desires are produced by vested interests outside the individual.

We pose this fundamental question: To what extent does a person have free choice regarding the desires that not only emerge within him, but become a part of his self-identity? If his free choice is the satisfaction of his desires, then do not his desires dictate the direction his free choice will take? *But what dictates what his desires will be in the first place?*

The Case of Elizabeth Van Dyke

Elizabeth Van Dyke, who a few months ago became a member of the International Society for Krishna Consciousness, is steadily being drawn into a program of chanting, working for the temple, praying long hours, collecting money on the streets, and listening as devotees of the Society inform her that her parents do not truly love her. If and when it is time for her to marry, Elizabeth will be wed to someone selected for her. If she expresses any interest in living outside the temple and away from her fellow Hare Krishna believers, she will be told that in making such a move she risks spiritual death. If she is caught talking about tennis, geography, friends on the "outside," or any other topic not connected with the teachings and duties of Krishna Consciousness, Elizabeth will be warned that such talk is a luxury in which devotees do not participate.

We will not elaborate further on the details of Elizabeth's new commitment. What we wish to ask is this: Assuming that Elizabeth not only *wants* to engage in her new religious activities, but *desires* the kinds of arrangements and activities found in the Hare Krishna Society, then how did these wants and desires originate within her? How did they become a part of her personality? It is quite unlikely that before joining the Society she knew about each practice and step within the Society. It cannot, therefore, be said that when she initially joined she actually *desired* at that time to participate in each activity and phase of the Society. Such desires were created later, inside the fold of the Society.

Caused to Desire

It is one of the chilling facts of life that finite human beings have little to say about which particular desires and wants will spring up within them. Not only are they more or less passive centers in which new desires come into existence, they are rarely conscious of the process by which the new desires are generated within them. The crucial point about all this is the fact that the desires that emerge within a person become *a part of him or her*. They are not merely something he is connected with, but rather they are vital *ingredients* of his own being. Without desires, he clearly would be nothing.

It is one thing to say that all our desires are caused and conditioned. But it is altogether another thing to say that all our desires come about under *compulsion*. Our desires as a whole emerge compulsively within us only if we prefer death as an escape from all desiring.

Most of us, however, discover that we do not desire extinction of all desiring. We discover, further, that only *some* of our desires exist under compulsion. And even in those cases, the compulsion is relative. What makes one desire compulsive is its persistency in the face of another desire (or set of desires) in severe conflict with it. For example, Charles' persistent desire for desserts is compulsive only to the extent that it is in severe conflict with his strong desire to control his weight and cholesterol count. It is necessary, however, to appreciate the *relativity* of compulsion. The strong desire to control one's weight and cholesterol is itself compulsive when viewed from the angle of the strong desire for desserts.

There is no freedom *per se*, no absolute freedom. It is always relative, which is not to say that it is illusory. Power is always relative. There is no power *per se*, but only the power to do this or that in particular. This power is not an illusion even though, like freedom, it is relative and temporary. Charles gains relative freedom in eating the pecan pie because temporarily he satisfies his desire for desserts.

Relative to the desire for desserts, Charles gains a measure of freedom in eating the pecan pie. Relative to the desire for a trim body and low cholesterol, however, he loses freedom and becomes a slave of his own *desire* for desserts. Relative to his own desire for desserts, Charles ate the pie of his own *free choice*. But relative to the desire for a trim body and low cholesterol, he ate the pie under *compulsion*. Free choice and compulsion are, therefore, both relative and real human conditions.

Charles is not a slave to desserts themselves, since he actually desires them. Rather, he is a slave to the *desire* for desserts *if* he desires a trim body. If, however, he has no desire for a trim body and has no other strong desire that comes in severe conflict with his desire for desserts, then we could not say that he is a slave to his desire for desserts.

Freedom or free choice is *always* relative to the individual's own personal desires. Jane's desires cannot define what is freedom for Charles. She may impose her private desires by depriving Charles of the means to satisfy his desire. But while that may be a measure of freedom for her, it is not for Charles.

Of course, Jane may be instrumental in one way or another in *causing* Charles to *change* his desires. Religious conversion is to a large extent the process by which a person's desires are changed or exchanged for others. Any profound understanding of human freedom must include some insight into the shaping and creation of desires. Rocks and clouds cannot literally become free or enslaved for the simple reason that they have no desires. Only in a metaphorical sense are inorganic objects to be spoken of as free.

We have said that human freedom is the satisfaction of desire. We have argued that human desires are many and that freedom is relative to the many desires, some of which stand in conflict with one another. We have indicated also that desires come into existence and pass out of existence and that the process is the product of physical causes and conditions. Finally, we have argued that some of these causes and conditions are very subtle and are detected only through careful investigation and observation. Indeed, often the conditions are so numerous and complex as to defy a complete cataloging of them. Religious conversion is usually brought about by numerous causes and conditions that are subtly woven together in complex patterns. Our concern has been to bring to light some of the most important patterns of the conversion process.

How to Turn Freedom Into Slavery

Once a religious group develops a momentum and structure of its own, it tends to behave somewhat like an organism in search of food. The primary food of such a social religious organism is new members. In order to recruit new members, the religious group may set out to brand certain human desires as worthy only of extinction. If the religious group can generate within an individual a desire to be rid of some of his present desires, then the individual will accept the group's designation of him as a slave to this or that passion or strong desire. It is crucial to understand that an individual is a slave to a desire only as it stands in severe conflict with especially those of his other desires to which he himself steadily gives his approval. It is therefore important to learn how various groups generate in an individual not only new desires, but judgments of approval and disapproval of desires.

Substituting of Desires

Religions often speak of transforming a person's desires. In reality, they may be successful in generating new desires as replacements of present desires. At other times, an old desire may have been extinguished by some form of social punishment. For example, if a new convert still has a strong desire to keep in close touch with family and old friends, his religious group may punish this desire by flooding him with fear-statements or guilt-statements. In addition, the group may even be successful in persuading the convert to move away from friends and family so that he is cut off from all the social reinforcements that they offer him. *The major part of any conversion is the elimination or repression of certain desires and the generation of new and different desires along with new reinforcements for the new desires.* The "old man" or the "old life" is largely the old desires and their system of supports.

We have not attempted to argue that religious conversion is good—or bad. Rather, we contend that it is a part of being a human being. This, then, leads us to discuss the fact that a conversion is more likely to come to a person when his desires are either (1) receiving minimum satisfaction or (2) in severe conflict with one another. There is, in addition, (3) a third condition that may bring about a conversion. It is the appearance of a new desire or cluster of desires in the individual's life. This new desire, far from being carefully articulated by him, appears only as a sharp rise in his expectations.

This third condition in particular has been considerably neglected in the study of religious conversion. A number of individuals clearly do come upon a period in their lives when they want and desire much more of life. At the very least they want a stirring new venture, a new and meaningful direction. If a religious group happens to encounter the individual at this time, he may find the religion to be "the answer" to his new surge of expectation. Or he or she becomes involved, not with a new religious group, but with a new friend of the opposite sex. The point here is that religious conversion need not in every case portray the old way of life as either evil or unworthy of human commitment. More positively, the conversion may be seen as human vitality claiming its new lease on life. It is a new birth of celebration, hope, and expectation. The "old life" is seen not as the Wicked City from which to flee, but as a part of one's personal continuity and heritage.

In their paper—"A Role Theory Interpretation of Deprogramming"—presented at the 1980 meeting of the American Academy of Religion, Anson Shupe, Jr. and David Bromley indicate that an individual may convert or reconvert by doing no more than adopting a public role. They add that this role may prohibit certain private thoughts and desires from being expressed openly. We suggest that conversion comes always in degrees and in part. Frequently, a conversion will include a considerable change of *overt* behaviors with only limited change of such *covert* behaviors or psychological states (such as desires and private beliefs). Conversely, sometimes an individual's covert feelings, beliefs, and desires will change even without a corresponding change in overt life-style or public behavior. (The covert spirit is willing, but the overt flesh is weak.)

Reconstructing the Memories of the Old Life

Very often, when an individual converts to a new religion, he does not hate his old way of life until his religious group teaches him to hate it. The religious group may even go so far as to teach the convert to reconstruct the memory of his old life in such a way as to make it less worthwhile than it actually was. Those religious groups that practice such reconstruction of the past do so largely out of fear that the new convert will not give absolute and total commitment to their new way if another way provides some joyous memories or exciting promises.

Our study of extramarital affairs in comparison to religious conversion reveals that quite often a person in an affair will begin to portray his or her spouse in negative words that are not entirely accurate or justified. As if to justify the new venture, he or she begins to degrade the earlier relationship. Similarly, there is in some religious conversions a kind of exclusivistic zeal that forbids the convert from even "flirting" with any other religious orientation or appreciating the commendable qualities of another faith. The new conversion is seen as a kind of marriage, and every association with other faiths is seen as religious adultery.

The point of comparing religious conversion with romantic passion or involvement is twofold: (1) to determine whether they have at some points an important common psychological condition and (2) to gain insight into the structure of religious conversion by exploring some of the structure and patterns of romantic involvements.

Romantic Passion and Religious Conversion

For a number of years we have been keeping notes on some revealing similarities between people in the throes or state of romantic passion and those in the throes of a new religious conversion. In Chapter 1 we noted that when in either of these two states, people are strongly reluctant to entertain even modest suggestions that the object of their love or commitment might be other than flawless.

But before going into other similarities, we offer the conjecture that there is a common "something" at play in both the new religious conversion and the new romantic involvement. At the risk of sounding mystical, we will use the phrase *élan vital*, or vital thrust, to refer to this something. It is "a thrusting and pushing and flinging of itself forward and an expansion outward to which no limit can be set."[1] We conjecture further that there is a strong biological base to this *élan vital*. Accordingly, it is the inner working of the body converging to open itself to a new kind, pattern, and intensity of reinforcers. In more popular terminology, the human body is undergoing a new surge of restlessness. The old life-style with its old support system will not suffice. The body moves toward a state of wildness—as if seized by a fit, at random until eventually the brain is forced to produce images, fantasies, or even what Carl Jung called archetypical myths. We do not wish to become as

---

[1]B.A.G. Fuller, *A History of Philosophy*, 2 vols.; 3rd ed., rev. by Sterling M. McMurrin (New York: Holt, Rinehart and Winston, 1960), 2:529.

mystical in this theory as Jung became, since we stress the biological base of the whole process. Nevertheless, the Jungians have placed their finger on something of major psychological and social importance.

It may very well be that universally—in every tribe, village, and city—certain common myths are projected by human beings. Our suggestion is not that these myths necessarily reveal the secrets of the cosmos, but that they have literally a *vital* function for the human species. This function is not to reveal theological and metaphysical truths, but to stir and move—literally—the human body in new directions. In that sense, the myths are transcendent in their power to cause people to step beyond their encapsulated condition. Doubtless, the myths can be wild and bizarre. But no matter, for that may be what is required to "inspire" and move human individuals and societies to fling themselves beyond themselves. The myths *involve* the human organism, stimulate it, arouse it, and sometimes even throw it into fits and insane behavior. Plato could speak of the "divine madness." People are sometimes said to "go crazy with love." They become "possessed" by love of woman or man, love of god, or love of the vision and myth.[2]

Our conjecture, then, is that the human organism under a variety of conditions becomes exceedingly restless and cannot be satisfied until it becomes passionately involved with some powerful myth, cause, god, hero, man, woman, war, or vision. Augustine was correct to speak of the restless human heart, but he was, we believe, mistaken to designate his own particular myth to be the one and only true answer to everyone's restless heart (or, as we would say, restless body and brain). Nature is "tolerant" of a variety of myths, though not infinitely tolerant.

It is not surprising that men and women have flings or even become powerfully involved in new romantic affairs, new religious causes, or new wars. What is surprising is that the cultural and social controls on this wild side of the human organism are as effective as they are. We suggest that the totem, god, and pantheon of a people represents the coming together of, on the one hand, the individual's restless and bold imaginative thrust forward via new involvements and myths and, on the other hand, the controls that the collective society and culture exert on these private ventures. The society and culture serve as a selective environment dealing with the Dionysian mutations that the "gifted" individual organisms project, as if by either divine imperative or demonic lust, but in actuality by biological necessity.

---

[2]See Joseph Campbell, ed., *Myths, Dreams, and Religion* (New York: E.P. Dutton, 1970).

Irresistible Grace

We now wish to note that in romantic passion or religious conversion, the individual seems to have been caught up or swept away. This is a way of saying that he appears to have been almost helpless to resist what has happened to him. So-called "love songs" tell of how people are swept off their feet or are rendered helpless to resist the love and influence of the beloved. Augustine could speak of his conversion in terms of "irresistible grace." New lovers are said to find each other irresistible. In one modern love song the lover confesses that he *can't help* falling in love with his beloved.

This phenomenon of feeling swept against one's expectations is, we believe, a kind of newness or freshness that surges forth in the individual's consciousness. At an unconscious level, various new expectations have been coming into existence and new alignments have been formulated, when suddenly the process breaks forth at the level of conscious feeling. And it comes as something of a surprise. The convert or the lover is surprised by joy!

Flings

The new directions that men and women take in romantic involvements may be defined by their relatives as flings. In some cases the flings are encouraged and regarded as harmless. In other cases, they are practically required, whereas in still other cases they are condemned. In some cultures, the fling that a married man or woman has may persist despite the strong disapproval of the society. Why? Morton Hunt in *The Affair: A Portrait of Extra-Marital Love in Contemporary America* offers an explanation: "It offers renewal, excitement, and the continuance of personal rediscovery."[3] The noted family therapist, Virginia Satir, told the convention of the American Psychological Association that "almost any study of sexual practices of married people done today reports that many married partners do not live completely monogamously. . . .The myth is monogamy. The fact is frequently polygamy."[4] Without disputing this, we would add that if the practice of shades and styles of polygamy in our culture is a fact, it is a fact dependent considerably on the upsurge of powerful fantasies and myths. The fling has been virtually institutionalized in some societies, whereas in others it functions as a kind of risk-taking adventure. Indeed, the fling is multi-functional. Our point is that very often relatives

---

[3] (New York: World Publishing Company, 1969), p. 22.

[4] Cited in ibid., p. 12.

and friends regard an individual's new religious conversion to be only a fling—a temporary venture, perhaps a foolish move, even an embarrassment to those who love him or her. Sometimes the religious fling, like the romantic fling, lasts for a short while and then fades away. But this may not mean that the religious fling was a mere epiphenomenal incident, since at its peak of intensity it may have "saved" the convert, not from eternal hell, but from a local hell of depression or "meaninglessness." Or it may have simply given him or her a new opportunity to gallop into the future with new hope and vitality.

Nothing Is the Same

In a moving song, Barbra Streisand sings that *nothing is the same* after her love has touched her. With a slight variation of the words, this powerful "love song" could be sung very effectively and appropriately at religious revival meetings and evangelistic crusades. If the "He" were clearly identified with Jesus in the song, the anticipating audience could find the song very meaningful—even thrilling—to them. Indeed, the record on which Streisand sings this song reveals a very large and jubilant audience in the background, not unlike the spirit of a rousing, stirring religious revival meeting.

Religions have often functioned to persuade individuals to believe that their lives need not be what they were. When Jesus or the African god Poro touches the individual's life, then "everything is new." The dead hand of the past loses its grip. "Therefore, if anyone is in Christ, he is a new creation; the old has passed away, behold, the new has come" (II Corinthians 5:17 RSV). In the exaggerated language of romantic passion or the new conversion, "nothing is the same."

The following might have been spoken by an evangelist regarding his conversion: "This is the moment from which things will date...." In fact, it is the expression of Neal Gorham, who had become passionately and romantically involved with Mary Buchanan. Neal told his counselor that he was "unable to believe what was happening, what might come to pass: the thing I thought I would never do, and *after which I will never be the same*."[5] Neal continued: "This is the moment from which all things will date; this is even now being woven into thousands of invisible connections in each of our brains, a network of memory in which we are forever caught; *we will never be the same again*."[6]

In a sermon entitled "The New Birth," Billy Graham said,

---

[5]Cited in ibid., p. 100. Italics added.

[6]Ibid., p. 101. Italics added.

I heard about a man some time ago who had been born again in
an evangelistic service. He was known as the city drunk. He was
called "Old John." Somebody spoke to him the next morning on
the street and said, "Good morning, Old John."
He said, "Who are you talking to? My name is not Old John. I'm
new John." A complete revolution had taken place in his life.[7]

There are equally moving testimonials of people whose lives have been
drastically changed by "falling in love," by marriage, or by some other form
of powerful romantic involvement. Because of the involvement, they are
today not the same persons they once were. The following is Roy's account
of a permanent change in his life:

My affair with Fran was completely different. I had never been
emotionally involved. It opened up things in me that had always
been closed off. . . . I'm not sure I could stand being opened up
like that twenty-four hours a day, but I'm very lucky I had the
experience. It left me permanently changed.[8]

Morton Hunt, who has interviewed numerous people in extra-marital
affairs writes: "Evidently, for certain kinds of people, even an
unconsummated affair can have significant consequences and be a
powerful force in one's emotional evaluation. It may be a liberating and
enlarging experience or produce constricting guilt and depression."[9] This
last sentence could have been, and actually has been, written about a variety
of religions, from liberal and conservative to Judaism and Hinduism. One
woman tells of her affair, so that with only slight changes the following
might have been spoken as a religious testimonial at a devout religious
gathering:

My outlook on life was completely changed by what happened.
The affair made me aware of my own need to think and to
communicate with someone I am deeply in love with. Before, I
was asleep; ever since, I have been awake.[10]

We are reminded of the words of the hymn: "I once . . . was blind, but now I
see."[11]

Of course, there is the factor both in romantic involvement and in
religious conversion of coming down out of the clouds or from the

[7]Billy Graham, *Peace with God* (New York: Pocket Books, 1965), pp. 127-28.
(Originally published in 1957 by Doubleday.)

[8]Cited in Hunt, *The Affair*, p. 272.

[9]Ibid., p. 93.

[10]Cited in ibid.

[11]*Amazing Grace*, by John Newton (1779).

mountain. One of the most painful experiences that human beings can undergo is that of losing the "spell" that the conversion or the romantic passion has cast over their lives. Indeed, in some cases the end of the spell brings hostility and even bitterness.

But for numerous others, bitterness never comes, or if it does, it fades in time, giving way to the memory of that time of joy and intensity which once was. Because of life's changes for both good and ill, the old love or the old faith can no longer be a reality, but it burns still as a flame in the heart. There is the memory of how the love, or faith, had changed their hearts and lives, as if nothing could ever again be the same. At the end of the story of *Camelot*, King Arthur tells the adventuresome little boy to flee the war and return home to tell of Camelot:

> Each evening from December to December,
> Before you drift to sleep upon your cot,
> Think back on all the tales that you'll remember
> Of Camelot.
> Ask every person if he's heard the story;
> And tell it strong and clear if he has not:
> That once there was a fleeting wisp of glory
> That was known as Camelot.
> Don't let it be forgot
> That once there was a spot,
> For one brief shining moment
> That was known as Camelot.[12]

It is significant that, in at least Western culture, no themes move and inspire musicians to write their songs more than do the themes of either religion or romantic involvement. Since human organisms must move and stir if the species is to survive, religion and romantic passion must serve to inspire and stir the musicians, whose music in turn stirs and moves men and women both inside their bodies and overtly. Indeed, there is a crucial interplay between music and romantic passion as well as between music and religious experience. Thanks to the bards—ancient and modern—the memory of the lost love and the lost faith is kept alive—as if to kindle yet another love, another faith.

Everything Looks Different

There are countless "love songs" which tell of how nature and the world look different now that the lovers have found one another.

---

[12]Alan Jay Lerner, *Camelot* (New York: Chappel and Company, 1960).

There were bells on the hill,
But I never heard them ringing;
No, I never heard them at all
Till there was you.
There were birds in the sky,
But I never saw them winging;
No, I never saw them at all
Till there was you.
And there was music,
And there were wonderful roses.

· ·

There was love all around,
But I never heard it singing;
No, I never heard it at all
Till there was you.[13]

A former member of the Unification Church writes of the changes in the new convert:

> Paul T., having accepted the "truth" of the *Divine Principle*, said that he found nature to be more beautiful and full than he ever had before. He felt life, saw color, and felt love of God in the natural world. What had been a mere setting became God's dwelling place, and he felt himself to be a part of its harmony and beauty.[14]

The American evangelist D.L. Moody relived and retold a thousand times the ecstasy of his "conversion to Christ":

> I went out of doors and I fell in love with the bright sun shining over the earth. I never loved the sun before. And when I heard the birds singing their sweet songs in the Boston Common, I fell in love with the birds. I was in love with all creation.[15]

To be sure, the sun and birds, and even the Boston gardens had been there before his conversion. And while Moody had seen them, he had not *really seen* them until there was Christ in his life.

Charles Colson tells of seeing things anew after his new birth:

---

[13]*Till There Was You*, by Meredith Willson. © 1950, 1957, Frank Music Corporation and Rinimer Corporation.

[14]Mark Savad, *The Unification Church and Conversion*, paper presented at the 1977 annual meeting of the American Academy of Religion (San Francisco).

[15]Quoted in Richard E. Day, *Bush Aglow: The Life Story of Dwight Lyman Moody* (Philadelphia: The Judson Press, 1936), p. 65.

As we drove into the city, . . . I also noticed how green and beautiful were the trees and shrubs lining the sides of George Washington Parkway, how clear and blue the sky. The outline of the city was suddenly before us as we rounded the great curve following the Potomac River: the white marble and glass of the building glistening in the sun, with the majestic Capitol Dome perched atop a knoll as a backdrop.

"That's quite a sight, isn't it, Stocton?" I remarked and then noticed the puzzled expression on the chauffeur's face as he glanced back at me through the rearview mirror. It was precisely the same view that had been there every morning all the months Stocton drove for me.[16]

The new birth—whether in romantic involvement or religious conversion—leads to seeing the same world in a different way. And yet it is more than that. The objects of the world are not exactly *the same* objects they once were. To see them in a different framework means that they are not exactly the same entities that they were in the old framework. A person "could point to the moon and the stars and call them *moon* and *stars*," but he might see them now as "expressions of the divine Being." One line of a romantic song goes as follows, "I'll be looking at the moon, but I'll be seeing you."[17] As is well-known, in some cultures lovers see the moon and the stars in terms of their own intense and personal relationship. The celestial bodies are somehow involved in the scheme to bring the lovers together to fulfill their destiny together.

Jonathan Edwards in his *Personal Narrative* writes the following account of his own religious experience:

After this, my sense of divine things gradually increased and became more and more lively, and had more of that inward sweetness. The appearance of everything was altered; there seemed to be, as it were, a calm, sweet cast, or appearance of divine glory, in almost everything. God's excellency, his wisdom, his purity and love seemed to appear in everything; in the sun, moon, stars; on the clouds, and blue sky; in the grass, flowers, trees; in water and all nature; which used greatly to fix my mind. I often used to sit and view the moon for continuance;

---

[16]Charles Colson, *Born Again*, pp. 146-47; see James W. Jones, "Reflections on the Problem of Religious Experience," *Journal of the American Academy of Religion*, 40: 4 (December, 1972), 447.

[17]"I'll Be Seeing You," words by Irving Kahal, music by Sammy Fain; from "The Royal Palm Revue."

and in the day spent much time in viewing the clouds and sky, to
behold the sweet glory of God in these things.[18]

Many a lover has sat looking at the moon, stars, clouds, and flowers
while dreaming of the beloved. The words, "All nature sings, and round me
rings/The music of the spheres" are found in a hymn.[19]But they could as
easily be sung by a lover as by worshipers of God. Indeed, many songs of
love resemble songs of worship. Lovers speak of "adoring" and
"worshiping" one another. Of God and lover, it is often said, "You are my
all." "All I need is you." There is even the element of thanksgiving and
gratitude. Of her affair, one young woman said:

> And then—I couldn't believe it—it was happening, it
> *happened*! I started laughing and crying, crying and laughing,
> and I couldn't stop. I kept thinking, "I'm complete. I'm a normal
> woman after all," and I said to him, "Bless you, bless you, for
> what you have given me."[20]

A Fool for Christ

The woman's exclamation, "Bless you, bless you, for what you have given
me," will cause some people to say, "The poor woman is making a total
fool of herself." Indeed, years later she may look back and say, "How could
I have been so foolish." By contrast she might look back and say, "I was a
fool in the eyes of those who did not understand; but fool though I may
have been, it was for me a chance to live, to come alive, to bring into being
a part of me that had never before been born. For me, it was a kind of
birth."

Indeed, one man entertained the thought of giving up his involvement
with a woman before it became uncontrollable. But he could not bring
himself to do it. He asked,

> How could I repudiate the person I had finally become? Give
> up the love that I had only begun to know? Turn away from
> the new life I had scarcely tasted? A retreat back to the torpor,
> the flatness, the dessication of my former ways, would be an
> imprisonment for life, with only my few recollections as a tiny
> window through which to look out upon the dear lost world.[21]

---

[18]Cited in James W. Jones, "Reflections on the Problems of Religious Experience,"
Journal of the American Academy of Religion 40:4 (December 1972): 445.

[19] Maltbie D. Babcock, "This is my Father's World," in *Thoughts for Every Day Living*
(New York: Charles Scribners, 1901).

[20]Cited in Hunt, *The Affair*, pp. 121-22.

[21]Cited in ibid., p. 188.

It is easy for us and our readers perhaps to sit in judgment of this man. But it is imperative to see that the man's passionate involvement with the woman was itself a form of religious conversion! In fact, the woman confessed, "Loving him, I was like someone who had just had a religious experience; how could I not believe?"[22] Think of all the money and all the social and cultural supports that converge to keep the members of respectable religions attached to these religions. Then think of how little money and how *few* are the social and cultural supports that this man and woman enjoyed as they came together in their affair. Like an intense religious community, they stood alone against the world.

Realizing that he and some of his fellow Christians were considered to be fools because of their religion, the Apostle Paul boasted of being counted a fool for Christ: "We have become a spectacle to the world, to angels and to men. We are fools for Christ's sake" (I Corinthians 4:9-10 RSV). Like illicit lovers, Paul sometimes saw himself and his fellow apostles as in disrepute before the wider society: "When reviled, we bless; when persecuted, we endure; when slandered, we try to conciliate; we have become, and are now, as the refuse of the world, the offscouring of all things" (I Corinthians 4:12-13 RSV).

Countless Hindus, Christians, Buddhists, and others have given up their businesses, their secure family positions, their money, and any number of other-worldly advantages in order to follow the god, the Path, or whatever. Lovers both inside or outside marriage have sometimes sacrificed worldly goods in order to do what outsiders said only fools would do. One man said, "For a man like me, the whole thing was crazy, absolutely crazy. . . . I had been making a hundred thousand a year, and here I was letting my business fall apart and making only a half or a third that much."[23]

Buddha is commended for having left wife, children, position, money, home, and friends in order to pursue salvation. Was he a fool? If a man finds a finite salvation or at least fulfillment with a woman, is he a fool to forsake all to pursue her? There is no neat answer. The point is that there is something in religious conversion and romantic involvements that is so profound, so deep, that at times men and women will forsake so much for faith or love as to be regarded by outsiders as obvious fools. It is surprising that more in-depth studies by social scientists have not been made of

---

[22]Cited in ibid., p. 189.

[23]Cited in ibid., p. 183.

powerful romantic passion in comparison with powerful religious conversion.*

Since the days of Voltaire at least, religious passion has been described as something which would eventually be eliminated from the human race because it would prove useless. There is no realistic basis to expect this to come about. Rather, the need is to understand it in depth, and it is hoped that this book has been a contribution in that direction. Indeed, despite predictions that romantic involvements would perish, we see no basis for these predictions either, but instead suggest that romantic passion be studied more thoroughly regarding the deep needs it meets and desires it fulfills. We predict that an extraordinary overlapping would be found in the study of religious conversion and romantic involvements. Each of them touches the deepest passions of the human heart.

Guilt and the Loss of Commitment

Because of guilt, young men and women have sometimes failed to break their publicly announced engagements to be married. Despite coming to believe that the marriage would not be a good one, some people have continued out of guilt. Some friendships are continued, not because they are rewarding and mutually supportive, but because of a sense of guilt in letting the friendship die. Some people have remained in a religious group, not because they find it rewarding or true or meaningful, but because of a sense of guilt. The minister may have married them or buried their father or mother. A Sunday School teacher may have been a friend in time of need. To cut themselves away from the church or the faith may be to create more feelings of guilt than they can bear. Indeed, there are grown men and women who have never told their parents that they have left their parents' religion or denomination to join another.

There is also the guilt related to the perceived concept of God. If a person changes drastically his view of God, does he at a deeper emotional level feel that he is exchanging his father for another father? Is he a father-murderer—psychologically?

There is also what has been called *existential guilt*. It is a kind of dread of death. To change one's religious commitment is in some way to die to the old commitment. But this opportunity to change creates what Reinhold Niebuhr called the "dizziness of freedom," which comes when the old is dead but the direction of the new commitment is not set forth with

---

* Since making this statement, we have discovered a new study of being in love, by Dorothy Tennov, *Love and Limerence: The Experience of Being in Love* (New York: Stein and Day Publishers, 1979).

certitude. This existential guilt is the felt remorse at having to cut loose from what has been a part of oneself.

Lovers have agonized over whether to end their relationship. Religious believers have agonized also. To move forward in one direction of religious commitment is to say "No" to another direction. To say "No" may be felt by some as an act of killing or destroying something. The wistful last look at that lost island wells up as existential guilt in the believer who adopts a new faith. Sometimes fanaticism is required by some new converts if the old involvements are to be eliminated from the mind.

In a recent study of Catholic Pentecostal prayer groups, a sociologist observed in seven such groups that the process of induction into each of these groups included the new members' acts of giving *testimonials*. This, rather than speaking in tongues, was the required act—the bridge-burning act.[24] Individuals vary in any religious group as to the acts and rituals they can participate in. Some groups give believers options. But there are times when a member can, for whatever reason, no longer in good faith participate in the required act. Yet he may continue to practice it in bad faith. This is very much like former lovers who carry out certain words and acts but not in good faith. There is a guilt that plagues both lovers and religious believers who cannot put their covert hearts in the required overt acts and words. If such guilt continues unalleviated, it may corrupt their love or faith.

The point is that members can sometimes suffer more than one kind of guilt or more than one source of guilt in their involvement in the religious group. This guilt factor, much of which is covert behavior, is very difficult to detect by casual observation. In-depth interviews are perhaps the most effective method for uncovering the forms of guilt that we have considered in this section. Whether or not religious groups can find and institutionalize methods for uncovering this guilt, and dealing with it without threats, remains to be seen. It may be that *some* churches maintain a large enrollment because they lack any humane method for letting go of those members who no longer have strong private commitments, even though their public commitment seems unchanged except perhaps to all but the trained observer. Like Pharoah, these churches will not let the people go into their own land of promise.

---

[24]See Meredith B. McGuire, "Testimony as a Commitment Mechanism in Catholic Pentecostal Prayer Groups," *Journal for the Scientific Study of Religion* 16:2 (June 1977), 165-68.

Hope and Commitment

Psychiatrist Victor Frankl, imprisoned in a concentration camp during World War II, noted that the prisoner who lost faith in the future was doomed, mentally and physically. One day at the prison, a man revealed to Dr. Frankl a strange dream that he had had in February 1945. In March he was full of hope because the dream had given him an answer. In February, the man had heard a voice in his dream, a voice which told him that he could wish for something. The man immediately asked the voice when the prison camp would be liberated and the sufferings of himself and his associates ended.

"What did your dream voice answer?" asked Frankl.

"March thirtieth," the man replied.

On March 29, one day before the day of deliverance was prophesied to come, the man became ill and ran a high temperature. On March 30, he became delirious and lost consciousness. On March 31, he died, to all outward appearances by typhus.[25]

Dr. Frankl believes that the man's sickness came because of a sudden lowering of his body's resistance against the latent typhus fungus. This lowering of resistance came because of loss of hope that the predicted deliverance would come. Dr. Frankl tells of a sharp increase in the number of deaths at another time at the camp and contends that it was the disappointment and loss of a specific hope that had made the deaths more likely.[26] Philosophers are highly critical of religious promises for their lack of definiteness and precision. *Cognitively*, these religions have little defense of their loose way of talking and promising. But *emotionally* and ultimately physically there is some merit in making the hopes and promises either vague or remote.

When William Miller in the early nineteenth century gave a specific time for a Second Coming of Christ, he was (contrary to what some have said of him) more the scientist at heart than were some of his contemporaries of the faith. When the Second Coming failed to come about, he, like a self-respecting scientist, checked his material to see whether he had made his prediction accurately. Revising his prediction after concluding that he had misread the Bible, he ventured another strong, testable prediction. It failed again. Miller got the message and quit prophesying.

---

[25]Victor Frankl, *Man's Search for Meaning: An Introduction to Logotherapy*, trans. Ilse Lasch (Boston: Beacon Press 1962). pp. 74-75. This is a newly revised and enlarged edition of the 1959 edition of *From Death Camp to Existentialism*.

[26]See ibid., p. 76.

But the Jehovah's Witnesses picked up where Miller left off. Charles Taze Russell and his group of Witnesses set the year 1914 as the proper date for Christ's return. "Millions now living shall never die!" Unfortunately, they did die. Christ did not return.

But that did not put to rest the Second Coming. Rather some Christians claimed that Christ really did "come again"—only he did not come to earth. Instead, he moved from one part of heaven to another part, namely, the inner sanctuary. Here the device of vagueness and the surrender of testability gave the believers the freedom to continue to speak of Christ's coming in such a way that nothing—absolutely nothing—could count as evidence against the prophecy. Hope was once again restored—at a price.

Hope is essential to human life. Looking to the future is medicine to the body. But it can kill the body if the promised day of glory turns out to be merely another day. Most religions have learned over the years to make their most outstanding promises vague, or at least remote. Marxists no longer set dates for the demise of capitalism, although back in the 1920's Marxists in every cafe in France or restaurant in Austria could be heard predicting the impending end of capitalism. Those were the good old days when faithful Communists would put their prophecies on the line. Today, Communists, like most historical religions, have learned to prophesy with zealous vagueness.

However, such vague hopes are not sufficiently effective to keep any religion going full steam. That is why more concrete reinforcers are required. The religion that offers wild and fanciful promises at one level may, at another level, provide very practical fulfillments for its new members. Such fulfillments may range anywhere from helping members to find jobs (an effective practice among Mormons) to finding them new friends. John Wesley worried that those in his movement kept improving themselves economically, a factor which proved to be both effect and cause of the flourishing of the movement.

In romantic involvements, the factor of unrealistic hope may keep the relationship going on despite serious damage to it. Morton Hunt reports the case of a St. Louis businessman:

> Horrified and enraged that she is not at all what he supposed, he fights with her about it, demands that she be what he thought she was; she, in turn, is first wounded, then infuriated, at being found less than marvelous and ordered to improve. But as their clashes increase in intensity and frequency, so do their efforts to recapture the earlier illusion and satisfaction.[27]

---

[27]Hunt, *The Affair*, p. 197.

A person who has been involved with many dimensions of his life in a particular religious faith will usually not be able to walk away from it as soon as he discovers serious flaws in it. He may first wish to improve or reform it if he can. Sometimes, partial reforms are sufficient to make possible the continuation of the relationship. But the attempted reforms and adjustments can lead in the end to a break that is much more fierce and rough than an earlier break would have been. Like lovers who break apart with much travail, the individual and his church may end up hating one another.

In some cases, believers seem strapped to the particular religion they happen to be involved in. Their behavior is nothing less than an obsession. This is sometimes true even when the believer no longer embraces the premises of the particular faith with which he has become obsessed. Edwin's relationship with Jennifer might simply have faded, since he had grown disillusioned with her. But his personal need made him cling all the more. It was the need "to see himself as romantic, virile, free-spending, and beneficent."[28] We know a Catholic whose obsession to cling to a faith he could no longer believe in was in many ways like Edwin's obsession with Jennifer. He had an image of himself as a believer, and he could not imagine himself a believer within any other framework.

"I made myself believe everything she told me, despite all the evidence to the contrary."[29] These words were spoken, not by a Catholic about his Church, but by Edwin Gottesman about Jennifer Scott. It describes to a great extent John Henry Newman's relationship with his Church. Eventually, however, Newman was given a position of respect as a Cardinal, whereas Edwin received seemingly little reward for his efforts. A careful study of what Jennifer gave Edwin would have brought an outsider to conclude without delay that Jennifer was someone to avoid if at all possible. She was bad news from the start, and the news grew worse with each passing month. Slowly—very slowly—Edwin began to see what was happening to him.

> The whole thing sickened me. I could see that I was involved with someone who was a liar, a spendthrift, unfaithful, greedy, lazy—but when she hung around my neck and clung to me, or when we went out some place together and I had that big showy girl on my arm, I didn't care. . . . I was like a man in a poker game who's been losing and losing, and insists on playing for higher stakes because he has to win it all back.[30]

---

[28]Ibid., p. 228.

[29]Cited in ibid., p. 202.

[30]Cited in ibid., p. 203.

Ken Billington was the minister of a church whose members not only opposed his theology, but were segregationists. He prayed, worried, and tried vainly to stay in the church and to make it work. An onlooker might have said, "Can't he see that the relationship is doomed, that eventually he and his church will come to a bitter parting of the ways?" But Ken could not look at the facts. He had spent three years in the school of theology, where he trained to become a minister. It was his "calling." He would not—could not—look at the facts because, like a gambler who has already sunk a large investment at the table, he kept hoping that through some miracle or work of grace, the church and he would unite together in Christian harmony and a fruitful relationship. After leaving Jennifer, Edwin was able to say, "I wouldn't look at the facts. . . ."[31] And, today, Ken Billington can make the same judgment about his former relationship with his church. In time, he developed a new religious affiliation, one that gave him more freedom and challenge to do meaningful work with other people, which is, he now believes, his true religious "calling."

The Flirt and the Proselytizing Agent

We have in this chapter attempted to draw some parallels between romantic involvements and religious involvements. We think one of the most fruitful parallels is the control systems used to keep marriages from coming apart and the control systems used to keep the relationship between the individual and his religious involvement from coming apart. Some churches are quite hostile toward evangelistic appeals and proselytizing. This hostility seems to arise from the assumption that a religious involvement is like a marriage. That is, if the two participants—whether in marriage or in religion—cannot remain together in mutual respect, then let them be free to divorce. But let no one tempt them to become dissatisfied with one another. Let the flirt cease his or her flirting; and let the proselytizing agent go home. In short, the proselytizing agent is looked upon by many religious groups as a kind of flirt, tempter, or temptress. Indeed, the proselytizing agent seems to be classified with "home wreckers" or "marriage wreckers."

By contrast, the proselytizing groups have an altogether different self-image. They see themselves not as seducers and destroyers of meaningful relationships, but as bearers of glad tidings for those who need deliverance. To be sure, they think that since most people are unaware of their own need of deliverance, they must be made aware of it.

---

[31]Cited in ibid., p. 183.

From Faith to Faith

In the religious "divorce and remarriage," it is often the case that the individual seems to have learned little from his previous religious involvement, since he quickly finds another religion that has most of the fundamental problems of the faith from which he divorced himself. Indeed, it is one of the most perplexing problems of modern religious converts to find the religion that meets their needs, including the need for developing intellectual honesty as well as other virtues.

Sometimes, it appears that one traditional religion has more divergent opinions and more conflict *within* it than it has with certain other traditions outside it—at least in certain areas of belief and practice.

> [Lucien] Goldmann is willing to use the word "faith" of the Marxist attitude, and he sees a real continuity between Augustinian theology and Marxism, despite their differences on such issues as the actual existence of God.[32]

Professor Alasdair MacIntyre, who once called himself a Christian and wrote as a Christian until his conversion to another perspective, is now prepared to revise his position again in order to say the following, which we regard to be a very significant point to be considered in any treatise on conversion:

> Goldmann contributes to an urgent contemporary task, that of redrawing the lines. . . . It has become increasingly plain that whether a man calls himself a Christian, a Marxist, or a liberal, may be less important than what kind of a Christian, a Marxist, or a liberal he is. I remarked earlier that Augustinians and Marxists do differ after all about the existence of God; but they agree that whether God exists or not is a crucial question. In so doing they unite against both Christians of the Tillich-Robinson kind and liberals of a certain kind who think religion a matter of "private" life [only]. . . . Both Goldmann and Sartre call themselves Marxists, [but that] does not obliterate the gulf that separates their views.[33]

The point is this: when a person converts to a particular religious group, his old friends and family need not conclude that they will no longer have any influence on his religious life. In our interviews with converts to such groups as the Moonies, Mormons and evangelicals, we learned that

---

[32]Alasdair MacIntyre, *Against the Self-Images of the Age: Essays on Ideology and Philosophy* (New York: Schocken Books, 1971), p. 84.

[33]Ibid., p. 86. Words in brackets are added.

there is considerable diversity within each group. The new convert is not without potential for growth, revision, and thoughtful inquiry. The point is to restore and keep in good repair the lines of communication between "insiders" and "outsiders" so that each may learn from the other.

Chapter VIII

Brainwashing and Other Recruitment Methods

The Oakland Family

In 1980 Martin Irwin ("Mose") Durst was appointed by the governing board of the Unification Church (Moonies) as the president of the UC movement in America, replacing Neil Salonen. Durst, a Ph.D. in the humanities with social psychological/sensitivity group training, rose quickly to a position of prominence in the Unification Church because he and his Oakland, California group proved to be the Church's most effective agency in recruiting converts. Most of the criticism directed at the "brainwashing" methods of the Moonies has been triggered by the methods used by the "Oakland Family" on the West Coast. We now wish to spell out some of those methods.

The Oakland Family's first step is that of searching out and finding the most likely candidates or prospects. Candidates come largely from young men and women in their late teens or twenties. Shupe and Bromley suggest that at this age people have least to lose in experimenting with a new church or new life style. Parents quite naturally feel the loss as their own, perceiving themselves as forced to sit helplessly by to watch go down the drain their own investment of loving care, teaching, money, worry, and other dimensions of their own lives which they have sacrificed over the years for their children. Parents tend to see this drastic change in the lives of their offspring as loss rather than as the young person's experiment in living.

Mose Durst trained his Oakland Family recruiters to search for candidates in places where young people would more likely be found, for example, public parks, shopping malls, libraries, city streets, bus and train stations, and centers of countercultural activity, such as college campuses and certain key urban areas.[1]

After the missionaries or recruiters go to the key places, they look specifically for young people who manifest signs of being in transition or transience. A backpack is one such sign. Another is an individual alone in, say, an airport or bus station and who behaves as if uncertain as to where he is going now that he has arrived in the city. Often the signs of transience cannot be uncovered until conversation with the prospect is initiated. By talking with especially those in their late teens or twenties, the recruiter can learn whether an individual has just graduated from high school or college, is looking for a job, or is in transition in some other way.

The search-and-find-the-prospect method is usually followed by what we call the method of attitude fitting. It is at this point that the charge of "heavenly deception" comes into play. *Attitude fitting* is the practice of coloring or slanting one's message by adapting it to the receiver's biases or established attitudes. Politicians sometimes attitude fit by adapting their message so that it blends with the given audience's attitudes (both positive and negative attitudes). People who wish to persuade us to act a certain way or believe a certain thing will sometimes study our attitudes or settled biases and then take advantage of them.

> If they wish to sell us an idea or a plan of action, they may color it or describe it so as to make it look like a kind of thing our attitudes favor, or they may select, instead of the real arguments, the arguments that will appeal to us.[2]

West Coast Moonies in particular have used this method in recruiting new converts. Instead of saying, "I'm a representative of the Unification Church, and I'd like to talk with you about what our Church might have for you," recruiters have introduced themselves as workers for world peace or as someone desiring to interview them about some appealing topic. "Are you interested in a meaningful way of life?" is an example of one of the West Coast "come-on" questions. One of us in a shopping center parking

---

[1]See David G. Bromley and Anson D. Shupe, Jr., *"Moonies" in America: Cult, Church, and Crusade* (Beverly Hills: Sage Publications, 1979), p.172.

[2]See Winston W. Little and others, *Applied Logic* (Boston: Houghton Mifflin Co., 1955,) p.39.

lot in Knoxville, Tennessee was approached by a woman who looked to be about thirty years old.

"I'm collecting money for Christian missionary endeavors," she said by way of introduction. "Would you care to contribute?"

"What kind of missionaries? Presbyterians, Communists, Buddhists?"

"Just Christian."

"Are you a follower of the Reverend Moon?"

"Yes."

"How long have you been in the movement?"

"Ten years."

The above true account is an example of deliberately withholding relevant information and adapting the message to fit the presumed positive attitude of the potential contributor of money. In this case, the woman acknowledged to being a Moonie after being asked only once. Other recruiters, however, have either denied their connection with the Unification Church or given an evasive answer. In talking with especially mainstream Unification Church leaders, we have learned that such evasiveness and deception have been criticized by mainstream UC members. (Virtually every denomination has an internal division regarding what is proper and what is improper in recruiting new converts.)

The West Coast Moonies in particular wish not only to solicit money but to gain new converts. The third step (after the search-and-find-the-prospect step) is that of offering *an invitation and transportation* to the Oakland Family community center in the countryside about a hundred miles from San Francisco.

At the center, the fourth step is initiated. It includes meals, exuberant singing, getting-to-know-you questions, entertainment, lectures or slide shows. The plan is to "love bomb" the prospect, making him feel accepted and very special.

The fifth step is moved into gradually, as the prospect is enticed and invited into the extended workshop. From the first day of arrival at the pleasant rural locale of Booneville, the prospects experience a fast-paced program, deliberately designed to deprive the prospect of any time alone or any opportunity to critically evaluate what is going on. The Workshop intensifies the experience, emphasizing *total* participation in a nonstop series of activities. The "buddy system" proves to be a device for assigning an experienced Moonie to a prospect in order to "interpret" for the prospect what is taking place. The "buddy" also generates affective pressure and skillfully diverts all questions and comments of a negative nature that the prospect might have. Communion and solidarity are emphasized, and significant others outside the center are played down or even disparaged. Even phone calls to and from those outside the center have been strongly discouraged.

The Oakland Family has differed considerably from the East Coast Moonies in one major respect. The latter group introduces from the beginning pictures of the Reverend Moon and Moonie theology. The California Moonies, by contrast, lead the prospect to believe that the center is a kind of humanistic and socialization center of some sort. Moonie theology and the Reverend Moon's role in the religion are introduced gradually and with subtle design.[3]

We will not go into the further steps by which the Unification Church attempts to turn prospects into full-time members, since our controlling purpose here is to gain some insight only into the initial recruitment methods used in gaining converts. What will appear obvious to many of our readers is the marked similarity between modern advertising methods and the recruitment methods of some religious groups. Attitude fitting in particular is used by many institutions and organizations in the United States alone. Universities and the military branches have been known to make unrealistic promises to young men and women. "Heavenly deception" is nothing new to American religious denominations. The Southern Baptist Radio and Television Commission produces a "Country Crossroads" program designed to attract country music fans to religion. In April, 1980 entertainer George Hamilton IV appeared as guest host of the program. In an interview, "Hamilton said he likes the subtle approach the program takes to tell people about Christ. He called it a 'gentle way to get the word across.' " The interviewer concluded in an article, "So when Hamilton travels on concert tours or sings at the Grand Ole Opry or appears on 'Country Crossroads,' he's not just pickin' and grinnin', he's also singing for Christ."[4]

Some Moonies have argued that they have been forced to practice "heavenly deception" in order to overcome misleading and negative newspaper and television reports about them. In short, they see their practice of attitude fitting as a measure needed to counter the public prejudice directed against them. Any group having a strong interest in gaining a sympathetic hearing will tend to attitude fit, presenting its best face and hiding its worst. This may be fruitfully compared to the practice of dating and courting, in which the individual presents his or her "better

[3]See Bromley and Shupe, *"Moonies" in America*, pp. 172-78.

[4] Renee Wash, "Entertainer George Hamilton IV," *Baptist and Reflector*, 46:15 (16 April 1980), 6.

side" or "better self," hoping thereby to attract and keep the affections of the other person.

A Question of Degree

Forthrightness and honesty come in degrees, which is not to say that the difference in degree is insignificant. It is the crucial difference. The use of "counter measures" to gain a favorable hearing may be more justifiable than the practice of depriving new converts of the opportunity to an open inquiry into their new faith. The point needs to be spelled out.

Religious Indoctrination and Religious Education

Indoctrination is the method of instilling a particular body of either information or verbal responses into the candidate. Parents and school teachers necessarily employ this method when they train or drill their children in the multiplication tables, vocabulary, rules of grammar, and other such material. If the word "brainwashed" is to be used at all, we suggest that it refer to the social/cognitive process of indoctrination in its most *closed* form.

We will now introduce the concept of *temporary indoctrination*, knowing that it will likely be abused by religious groups who are fundamentally hostile to religious education but favor religious indoctrination. It may be necessary for families and religious groups to close the candidate off temporarily from critical questions and the attractions of rival beliefs until the family or religious group has assured itself that the candidate has gained a sufficient grasp of the favored doctrine or verbal material. This is, of course, indoctrination. We think it can be morally justified only if it is seen as a *preliminary step in education*. This means that indoctrination as an end in itself is morally unjustifiable. Or, stated with perhaps more practical realism, indoctrination in any area is not morally unjustifiable so long as the door is left open to future education in that same area.

Education must, by definition, remain open to both (1) critical analysis and (2) consideration of alternative positions and interpretations in any given area of inquiry. This is another way of saying that education is rational or *objective* inquiry. Education is not, therefore, the precise opposite of indoctrination. Rather, indoctrination is simply the first stage in education. Until the other stages are brought into the picture, education has been aborted. Indoctrination may be defined as education that has been aborted.

Loss in Either Indoctrination or Education

When the religious convert is given freedom to go beyond indoctrination to a more open religious education, he runs the genuine risk of seriously altering or even giving up the beliefs of his indoctrination. This is probably stated too mildly. It is *very likely* that he will not retain all the verbal responses of his original indoctrination but will at the very least expand and qualify them. Whether the qualifications will be classified as deviations or as enrichment depends on a variety of conditions which we cannot discuss in this book.

The risk of indoctrination alone is that of cutting the religious commitment off from intellectual development and depth. In a dynamic and pluralistic society, this is a most severe loss, since *moral* development is impossible without supportive intellectual development.

Ambivalence About Education

Almost all religious bodies suffer ambivalence regarding religious education. The Southern Baptist Convention is only one of several religious denominations having interest groups whose preference is that of indoctrination over education. We suggest that any religious group has a right to indoctrinate its students in a portion of the denomination's beliefs or tradition. But if there is indoctrination only, then the very structure of an educational institution is necessarily undermined.

Those who want indoctrination only face a crucial problem of self-conflict. On the one hand, they want at least the *reputation* of having centers of education for their children. On the other hand, they want to be guaranteed that their children at the college, or even at the seminary, will not significantly deviate from the beliefs of their original indoctrination. In short they want the feeling and reputation of education without running any of its risks.

Openness of Inquiry

We ourselves would prefer that the term "brainwashing" be eliminated because it is so misleading. But since it is currently in vogue, we suggest that it be defined in social/cognitive terms as simply that stage of indoctrination which is closed off to all objective inquiry. Objective inquiry, we repeat, is two-pronged: (1) openness to critical analysis of the material under study and (2) openness to examine other views, material, and interpretations.

In *Essay on Liberty*, John Stuart Mill in the nineteenth century suggested that a person's understanding of his own position will be severely limited unless he compares it to rival positions. But this entails looking into rival positions and running the risk of having one's thinking and life influenced by doing so. While many of us experience anxiety about the risk involved in objective or rational inquiry, we are made even more anxious by rumors of brainwashing, fearing that it will render us helpless, as no longer rational beings, deprived of both our critical capacity and our intellectual flexibility. In short, freedom that is essentially *human* freedom is perceived as necessarily linked to the capacity for rational inquiry. "Brainwashing" symbolizes the threat to sever that necessary link.

The Question of Brainwashing

In January 1979, at a Dallas radio station, one of us interviewed Henry Cha and Ed Stapleton about the Reverend Moon and his followers. Mr. Cha is the Texas director of the Unification Church and Mr. Stapleton is a Southern Baptist and an attorney who has, in the courts of Texas, successfully defended the civil rights of the Moonies.

Many parents have charged that the Moonies themselves are violating either the civil rights of young people or their human dignity by using brainwashing tactics. In the Dallas interview, Mr. Cha was asked whether the Unification Church has practiced brainwashing to gain converts from among the ranks of youths. He replied "no" and proceeded to charge that the deprogrammers, not the Unification Church, were guilty of practicing brainwashing. Cha argued that since physical force had not been used to restrain the new converts to the Unification Church, no one could truthfully claim that they had been brainwashed. In response to the question of whether the followers of Jim Jones had been brainwashed, Cha concluded that they had not, since no physical force had been used to make them board the ship that carried them to Guyana.

It must be said that no physical force of the conspicuous type that Cha had in mind was used by Jim Jones to induce his followers to drink the poison that killed them. In some sense, they drank it *voluntarily*. Yet there is clearly something about the methods used by Jim Jones that strikes many people as being beyond the pale of rational persuasion.

Can an individual be brainwashed even though no physical force—or threat of physical force—has been used to restrain or coerce him? Is it possible to use *psychological* restraint or control to effect drastic changes in an individual's personality and orientation? If it is possible, then is brainwashing to be seen as a special form of manipulation? These are difficult questions, partly because they involve us in the task of defining words that are highly charged with emotion. For some people, the word "brainwashed" implies the use of overt physical force. For others, it does not. Since we cannot bring about a public consensus of the use of this very controversial word, we will try to avoid becoming bogged down in a verbal skirmish. We do, however, advance the thesis that all the controls that influence and shape our lives are physical. Some of these controls are extremely subtle, whereas others are quite conspicuous.

We can offer an example of what we mean. If Bill has been lost in the desert for a number of days and is found by John, then John may be able to manipulate Bill simply by promising to give him water. This may be called *psychological* manipulation, but its ingredients and elements are all physical. Bill's biochemical state of deprivation is a physical state. John's canteen of water is physical, too, as are the sounds that John produces in the form of words of promise. To be sure, this kind of control or manipulation is more subtle than, say, using a pole or whip to compel Bill to behave in a particular way, but in both cases the controlling forces are physical.

When people are in a state of extreme deprivation—especially to the point of desperation—they are more easily manipulated to do what they might very well *not* do under less depriving conditions.[5] We suggest that some of the questionable tactics and methods used by various religious groups would not be successful if the subjects were not desperate or extremely deprived. Indeed, one of the paradoxes of religion is that while it is designed to come to the aid of people who are sometimes in a state of desperation, it is condemned if it takes unfair advantage of human desperation.

Brainwashing vs. Rational Method

A conversion may come about under either brainwashing conditions or rational conditions. Those are the two opposite poles on a continuum. Most human decisions are probably made somewhere between these two poles. It will not be easy to nail down a definition of either "brainwashing" or "rational" that is free of ragged edges. Nevertheless, we can in a preliminary way mark off what we mean by "rationality" as we reflect on what other people mean by it in their ordinary discourse as well as their more rigorous discourse.

It is useful to distinguish a rational method from a rational conclusion. What people profess to want to arrive at in their thinking is a rational rather than an irrational conclusion. But what the most rational conclusion is regarding a given issue may be a matter of debate. Nevertheless, even though people may not agree in advance on what the rational conclusion is, they may agree on a general process of working toward a rational conclusion, or at least communicating with one another about it. To this process we give the name 'rational method'. It is not our intention to

---

[5] For some very important articles on only one kind of deprivation—not to mention sensory overload of the brain—see Philip Solomon and others, eds., *Sensory Deprivation: A Symposium held at Harvard Medical School* (Cambridge, Massachusetts: Harvard University Press, 1961).

become involved in the fruitless controversy as to what *true* rationality is. We offer our preliminary meaning of 'rational method' and leave it open for criticism. But we would add that those who attempt to criticize it are themselves already in agreement with two of the first characteristics of "rational method" (or objective inquiry) that we propose.

First, to have a rational method in dealing with issues and questions is to *open one's view(s) to criticism*. This is not to predict that one's view will fall under the criticism. Rather, it is to say that to the degree that a person will not listen to or give careful consideration to the criticisms raised against the view in question, then to that degree he is not following a "rational method."[6] Of course, since there are other ingredients of the rational method, a person may be following the method in one respect but not in another respect. This leads us to the second ingredient of the rational method, an ingredient we mentioned earlier in this chapter.

It is an *openness to other views* having to do with the issue in question. To be thus open is not to predict that one of these other views might be a more rational conclusion than one's own. Rather, it is to admit that one or more of the views *might* turn out to be better. In practical terms, this means that to the degree that a person follows a 'rational method' of inquiry, he will devote a measure of time and effort to looking carefully at other views with a view toward understanding them in considerable detail. It means being open or listening to advocates—in print or in speeches—as they present their arguments. By "listening," we mean following the argument, which is to be distinguished from either believing it or rejecting it.

Brainwashing, Conversion, and Radical Shift

If brainwashing is anything, it involves the practice of closing off all criticisms of the view advocated by the group in control. To have control in this context means "having the power and means to shut off critical scrutiny of the favored view." In his book *Prisoner of Mao*, Bao Ruo-Wang notes how in a Communist labor camp he was prohibited from expressing any criticism of the Chinese Communist views. Furthermore, he was denied the means of studying, looking into, or openly discussing

---

[6]This ingredient of openness to criticism is discussed by a growing number of philosophers and social scientists: Tom Settle, "Is Scientific Knowledge Rationally Justified?" in W.R. Shea, ed., *Basic Issues in the Philosophy of Science* (New York: Science History Publications, 1976), pp. 28-29; Roger Trigg, *Reason and Commitment* (New York: Cambridge University Press, 1973); Robin Horton, "African Traditional Thought and Western Science," *Africa* 37 (1967), 50-71, 155-87; William W. Bartley III, *The Retreat to Commitment* (New York: Alfred A. Knopf, 1962), chapter 5; Paul K. Feyerabend, *Against Method* (Atlantic Highlands: Humanities Press, 1976).

views that were alternatives to those of the Chinese brand of Communism. Indeed, even the criticism he was encouraged to make of American imperialism and Soviet revisionism were the set criticisms that the prison administrators preferred and required. Furthermore, criticisms of these set criticisms were strictly prohibited and severely punished. The prisoner was permitted to engage in "self-criticism," which was a process of pointing out where he had not followed prison regulations or had not agreed with the administration. But he was not permitted to criticize the regulations or the views and ideas of the administration. When eventually Bao Ruo-Wang went along with this whole program of conditioning, he had become "brainwashed."[7]

Since the Korean War, the term "brainwashing" has called attention to the *speed* with which some people can have their political orientation changed. Ordinarily, people require *time* to think out the pros and cons and to follow the arguments involved in the issue. But brainwashing includes no genuine process of debate and rational discourse in which participants follow the rational method which we referred to above.

Sometimes "brainwashing" suggests a *radical shift* in one's view of orientation. Usually, such a shift is conspicuous because of the relatively brief time that it takes to come about. Over a ten year period a person's view may change profoundly, but it may not be as noticeable as the view of someone who had exchanged views within the period of, say, only a month. Delores at, say, thirty-five may embrace religious or political views radically different from the views she embraced when she was twenty-five. Indeed, Bill may change his views within a period of only a month, and the change of views may not be as radical as Delores' change. But Bill's will *seem* to be more radical because of the comparative shortness of the time.

Some people seem to think that a genuine conversion must be one that takes place suddenly.[8] This, we contend, gives an illusion of having supernatural causes behind it. People can more readily understand a change when it comes about over a considerable period of time. Because they can observe, or think they can observe, some of the natural and social conditions which seem to have brought about the change, some religious groups tend to regard such a change to be ordinary and not a genuine supernatural conversion.

Brainwashing seems to have something in common with the view that

---

[7]See Bao Ruo-Wang (Jean Pasqualine) and Rudolph Clelminski, *Prisoner of Mao* (New York: Coward McCann and Geoghegan, Inc., 1973), pp. 280-81.

[8] See Wayne E. Oates, *The Psychology of Religion* (Waco, Texas: Word Books, 1973), pp. 104-106.

a truly supernatural conversion must be sudden or quick. It has been a source of disturbance if not confusion for some Christian groups to have to face the fact that such groups as the Unification Church and the Chinese Communists in Korea have been able to "transform" a person's orientation within a remarkably short time. The dilemma which Christian groups must face is this: either (1) conclude that the drastic and quick transformations to non-Christian orientations are to be explained by causes and conditions that are not supernatural or (2) conclude that these non-Christian transformations are supernaturally caused.

If the first horn of this dilemma is accepted, then the question emerges as to whether *all* apparently quick and dramatic transformations are brought about by causes and conditions that are *not* supernatural. If the second horn of the dilemma is accepted, the consequences of the Christian conversion or new birth would seem to be undermined.

One way that some Christian groups have dealt with this second horn is as follows: the non-Christian transformations are indeed brought about by supernatural forces. Such forces are none other than Satan and his demonic followers, all of which have supernatural powers. The price paid for such a resolution of the dilemma is considerable: the natural, social, and cultural elements of life are simply ignored. All explanations are a form of reductionism, but this particular Christian view is a reductionism that throws us back into the Zoroastrian religion, which had two supernatural forces running the show, with the rest of the universe serving as mere shadows of the struggles and battles carried on by the two supernatural cosmic powers.[9]

Unfair Tactics and Methods

Various religious groups disagree with one another about what counts as fairness in their endeavors either to win converts to their own ranks or to prevent their own members from converting to another faith. Some officers of the Spanish Inquisition appeared to believe that the goal of saving a soul from hell could justify virtually any means, including torture. Other groups might be more inclined to use torture to convert an individual if they thought that genuine conversion (or genuine faithfulness) could be produced by torture. Most religious groups seem to hold, however, that a conversion is not genuine unless it is mediated in some sense through the individual's *free choice*. Unfortunately, in our

---

[9]See Joe E. Barnhart, "Reductionism and Religious Explanation," *Perspectives in Religious Studies*, 4:3 (Fall 1977), 241-52.

attempts to understand religious conversion, we will find few concepts as complex and complicated as the concept of free choice.

Conditioning, Conversion, and Brainwashing

There is something frightening in the thought that our children or we ourselves might be brainwashed by organizations that we regard as cynically manipulative. And even when the physical means of controlling and altering our behavior are in the hands of people we tend to agree with and trust, we still feel our finitude very strongly. We feel it just in thinking of how easy it is to influence and shape our behavior. Dr. Kenneth E. Moyer

> reports how "a mild-mannered female patient became aggressive, verbally hostile, and threatened to strike the experimenter when she was electrically stimulated in the region of the [brain's] amygdala. When the current was turned off, she again became mild-mannered and apologetic for her behavior. Her hostile behavior . . . could be turned on and off at the flick of a switch."[10]

Uncontrollable epileptic rage used to be regarded as an influx of supernatural spirits. Whether the spirits were considered good or evil was largely determined by the metaphysics and value system of those passing judgment. Neurosurgeon Vernon Mark reports the case of an engineer of high professional standing who was violent for a period of over ten years, during which time he often assaulted his family and endangered many lives by his dangerous driving habits.

> He suffered from seizures originating in the amygdala. "Stimulation . . . of the left amygdala produced a feeling of 'going wild' and 'I'm losing control.' On the other hand, [electrical] stimulation in the lateral amygdala, [merely] three millimeters away . . . produced a sensation of hyperrelaxation,' a feeling of 'detachment,' 'just the antithesis of my spells.' In his usual state, this patient was keenly aware of the slightest personal insult or threat, and his response was often sudden or violent. Under the effects of lateral amygdala stimulation, he showed bland acquiescence to the suggestions that the medial portion of his temporal lobe was to be destroyed." In this case,

---

[10]Perry London, *Behavior Control* (New York: Harper and Row, 1969), p.149, citing Kenneth E. Moyer, "Kinds of Aggression and their Physiological Basis," *Communications in Behavioral Biology*, abstract no. 08680058 part A, 2 (1968), 65-87. We have added the words in brackets.

ablative surgery was necessary, and once accomplished, the rage reactions disappeared.[11]

In other societies a similar transformation in personality might have been attributed to the power of Zande witchcraft, to the workings of the Virgin Mary, or of the healing power of Jesus or the Father. In India, if a similar transformation had come about, one of the deities would likely have received credit. Of course, if the transformation of personality is judged as bad, then various societies have various persons to "blame." Hindus regard certain designated deities responsible for evil; other groups blame such underworld persons as Satan or his evil underlings; still other groups blame the individual himself, or an aspect of him that has been labeled "free will." Because some Christians deny "free will" in the technical sense of the term, they may blame the individual himself as a *whole*. Or if it is not the whole of him, it is at least some *part*, such as the evil heart, the evil mind, or the evil desires. For still others, the causes may be somewhere inside the physical brain or somewhere in the conditioning process outside the individual altogether.

Free Choice as Always Conditional

Many persons seem quite reluctant to accept the conclusion that all human choices are conditional. In a recent television program, one of us was interviewed on the topic of the recruitment methods of the "cults." The interviewer kept insisting that those who join the "cults" do so without any free choice, whereas those who join the mainline churches do so of their own free choice. The interviewer seemed to think that either a person had free choice unconditionally or he had it not at all.

Rather than attempt to define free choice in any final way, we will indicate why it is that free choice is always conditional.[12] Each time a person selects one option over another, his choice is the product of numerous *conditions* that are both external and internal to his brain and body. This is but another way of saying that every human being is finite at every turn of his life. Whatever the differences between theologian Friedrich Schleiermacher and psychologist B.F. Skinner, they are in agreement that each human creature is *absolutely dependent*.[13]

---

[11]London, *Behavior Control*, p.149. We have added the words in brackets.

[12]See Jonathan Edwards, *Freedom of the Will*, ed. Paul Ramsey (New Haven: Yale University Press, 1957).

[13]For a brief sketch of behaviorism, see Richard I. Evans, *B.F. Skinner, The Man and His Ideas* (New York: E.P. Dutton and Company, 1968). Perhaps the best introduction to

We may go so far as to say that this state of absolute dependency is incurable. To be human is to be inescapably dependent on a network of countless conditions or contingencies. This view is not, however, to be confused with fatalism. It is necessary to be very clear at this crucial point. So long as a human being is alive, he cannot overcome his state of dependency. What he sometimes *can* change, however, is his dependency on a given type of condition. When people say that time sometimes heals, they correctly presuppose that over a period of time new conditions often enter an individual's life in such a way as to offset his dependency on some of the old conditions that are a source of injury or harm to him.

Freedom may be seen as the process of gaining release from certain conditions on which one does not want to be dependent. But that is freedom only in the negative sense of escaping from something. If we are able to be succesfully freed from certain conditions, we must find *new conditions* of another kind to replace the dissatisfying ones. That is fredom on its positive side. What is absolutely crucial to understand here is that freedom, in its most elementary and basic sense, is not escape from dependency per se. It is, rather, escape from *dissatisfying* conditions of dependency.

Free choice, therefore, is not the choice to be totally and absolutely independent. Our independence is always relative and conditional. All choices are relative and conditional. In a profound sense, the *independent thinker* enjoys his independence only because he is descipliined to be dependent on a certain kind of condition. This needs to be spelled out, especially since members of mainline churches are prone to think that anyone who joins a "cult" does so because he has been robbed of his independence of mind.

Independence of Mind

It is fruitful to ask what an independent thinker gains independence from. From what is he free? The answer is that he is free from the kinds of controls that interfere with his capacity both to follow an argument and to examine it critically and imaginatively. An independent thinker can focus on the issue without being *controlled* by appeals and causes that are irrelevant to the issue under examination.

But does this mean that the independent thinker is free from *all*

behaviorism is B.F. Skinner, *About Behaviorism* (New York: Alfred A. Knopf, 1974). Skinner wrote in a letter to us that he decided to write this book because of the widespread misunderstanding of his earlier book *Beyond Freedom and Dignity* (New York: Alfred A. Knopf, 1972).

controls? Not at all. He is *under the control* of the process of rational inquiry! If his thinking is not captured and controlled by his training in logic, critical investigation and imaginative speculation, he *cannot* be an independent thinker. When a person says that he was *compelled* to draw a certain conclusion, we interpret this to mean that the *force of the argument* was so strong as to make it relatively impossible for him as a rational person to draw any other conclusion. And if he moves later to a different conclusion, it will be because different arguments and evidence have entered into his thinking and because he is the sort of person who is largely controlled by rational debate and openness to evidence and logic.[14]

We do not wish to argue that anyone is *entirely* controlled by the process of rational investigation. Nor do we wish to offer a superficial description of this process. Our point is that if anyone is to avoid falling excessively under the control of irrational appeals and unfair tactics of "mind control," he must be considerably *under the control* of whatever those conditions are that make up the process of rational inquiry and informed investigation.

Later in the chapter, we will say more about the elements of rational inquiry in the conversion process. But we will now say more about our thesis that to be a human being is to come under various controls. Indeed, we wish to speak of freedom *by* or *through* controls. The failure to grasp the essential relationship between freedom and its controlling condition is, we believe, a major source of much confusion about the role of controlling conditions in the conversion process.

Freedom by Controls

Many Christians, Muslims, Hindus, Jews, and others who affirm belief in a God are eager to admit that they pray that their lives will be lived under the *control* of God. Paul the Apostle holds to the seeming paradox that to be a slave of the Lord is to be free (see I Corinthians 7:22). Furthermore, even though he warns against becoming "slaves of men" (I Corinthians 7:23 RSV), he speaks of himself as "a slave to all" (I Corinthians 9:19 RSV).

People have for centuries spoken and written of becoming slaves of passion, slaves of sin, slaves to the elemental spirits, and slaves to drink. Paul tells the Christians of Galatia that he is no longer a slave, but a son of God by adoption (see Galations 4:7). Only in certain passages does Paul consider slavery to be undesirable or at least a morally unacceptable state.

---

[14]See C. H. Whiteley, "Mental Causes," in *The Human Agent: Royal Institute of Philosophy Lectures, Vol. 1, 1966-67* (New York: St. Martin's Press, 1968), p. 105.

In other passages, however, he refers to himself and other Christians as slaves of Christ or God (see Romans 1:1, 13:4; Galatians 1:10; Colossians 1:7). To be sure, in these and other such passages, the new English Bible and the Revised Standard Version use the milder translation of "servant," although the RSV does use "slave" in the footnote as an alternate translation. It is noteworthy that in the RSV the word *doulos* is translated "slave" when Paul contrasts being a slave with being a son. It is also the same word *doulos* that is translated by the RSV as "slave" when Paul in Galatians 4:3 contrasts the Christians' present freedom with the time when they were "slaves to elemental spirits of the universe." In Galatians 4:9 he uses a form of *doulos* to point out that the Christians no longer want to be "slaves" of these elemental spirits.

In the light of our own study of Paul's use of *doulos* and its variations, we think it is misleading to translate *doulos* as "servant" rather than "slave." Within Paul's frame of reference, there is no contradiction between being free and being a slave of Christ. Furthermore, he even speaks of being "slaves of one another" (Galatians 5:13) as well as "slaves of righteousness" (II Corinthians 11—15). "For you were called to liberty, brethren; but do not use your liberty as an excuse for the flesh, but be slaves of one another through love" (Galatians 5:13, our translation).

In Paul's view, a person can be free and at the same time be a slave of Christ, of righteousness, and of fellow Christians. While we do not agree with Paul's supernaturalism, we nevertheless think that his understanding of the concept of freedom or liberty is quite realistic on at least one crucial point: Everyone's life is shaped by controls. The question, therefore, is not, "Can we escape controls?" Rather it is, "What controls will we live under and what controls will we not live under?" A piano player cannot be a player unless he is under the control of the musical score as well as other contingencies that make him a musician rather than a musical illiterate.

To be a life of any form at all is to be under a variety of controls. Some human lives are controlled considerably by alcohol. Others by the cues and reinforcements of their jobs. Others by voices. Others by what they read. Each individual person is controlled by a complex of contingencies and conditions. But the point is that to be a human being at all is to be shaped and directed by a vast display of controls, some of which are unique to the human species. For example, no horse or antelope can come under the control of the arguments of a rational discussion on the moral problem of abortion, on the problem of entering one's aged parents into a retirement home, or on a thousand and one other problems. But human beings can come under the control of arguments, both good and bad. They can have their lives shaped and directed by information, criticisms, evaluations, encouragements, interpretations, suggestions, and other social and logical "input" into their lives.

Free Choice and Human Dignity

If all the choices of a person are caused by conditions both inside and outside his brain and body, then can his religious conversion be the result of free choice? And if a person has no free choice in the first place, then why should any religious group be morally concerned about the tactics or methods it uses to convert him? Many people say that certain kinds of tactics are objectionable because they show no regard for human dignity. But if free choice is an illusion, then is not human dignity also an illusion? The fundamental question of this chapter may be asked in still another way: If there is no human dignity to take into consideration in the conversion process, then what is the point of condemning any religious group from using certain kinds of methods to win converts?

We seem to be faced with a very disturbing dilemma. (1) If we deny that our choices are controlled and conditional, we must conclude that they are random happenings void of any meaningful connection with our character or with our particular finite circumstances. (2) If, by contrast, we affirm that our choices are controlled and conditional, we must conclude that they are not free. What this dilemma boils down to is this: we can lay claim to freedom of choice *if* we are prepared to surrender our claim to having any rational understanding of our choices. These choices will be free but entirely beyond understanding in any degree and entirely disconnected from our personalities, our character, and our conditions. In fact, because such choices would be entirely independent of every condition and circumstance, they could not be *our* choices. They would be, instead, merely random events which happen to pass through us but which have no historical connections, causes, rhyme or reason.

Needless to say, this view seems to leave us as the victims of alien choices that both come upon us without warning and pass without meaning. Fortunately, there is an alternative position on human choice, a position that allows us to believe that there are free choices which are both (1) *our* free choices and (2) subject to controls and conditions. We have already offered a theory as to how this can be the case, and we will now elaborate.

Beliefs and Tactics

Earlier we suggested that the adult followers of Jim Jones joined him in Guyana and finally killed themselves voluntarily or of their own free choice. We have talked in depth with a number of people who belong to what the news media refer to as "cults." Our conclusion is that these people joined of their own free choice.

We will leave aside the question of whether or not the beliefs of any particular group are rational, since the issue in this chapter revolves around the *methods and tactics*.[15] Moving straight to the issue, we note that a person may freely select an option even though the conditions under which the choice was made were not conducive to rational inquiry and evaluation. The choice was free simply because it was what the individual *desired or wanted*. We sometimes forget that an individual's choice may be free even though unwise. Merely because it is free does not entail that the choice was arrived at through a rational process.

Let us take the case of Cynthia's conversion to the Unification Church. First, did she enter of her own free choice? Yes. Why? Because she *desired* to do so.

Second, is the belief-system of the Unification Church a rational system? That question is a matter of debate. We ourselves regard the theological claims of the Reverend Moon and his followers to be quite irrational to the point that we would be quite concerned if a large portion of the population should embrace them.

The third question, however, is the most important one to consider in this chapter. Are the recruitment tactics and methods of the Unification Church rational? That is, does the Church provide its recruit candidates an environment that strongly supports rational inquiry and objective examination of the Church's claims? We do not believe that it has done so in the past. In fact, there is good reason to think that in some of the Church's centers, new converts have been discouraged from raising certain relevant questions and expressing doubts about the Church's belief-system.

In fairness to the Unification Church, however, we should point out that many other denominations and religious groups—both mainline and fringe—have without shame severely repressed rational and intelligent inquiry in order to sweep new converts into their fold. Also, in fairness to the Unification Church, we wish to point out that its Unification Theological Seminary in New York does provide the students there with

---

[15]For a philosophical inquiry into the question of God's existence and related philosophy of religion topics, see J.E. Barnhart, *Religion and the Challenge of Philosophy* (Totowa, New Jersey: Littlefield, Adams and Company, 1975). For a more advanced study, see J.E. Barnhart, *The Study of Religion and Its Meaning* (New York: Walter de Gruyter, Inc., 1977).

an academic environment that strongly supports rational study and inquiry. Indeed, we find it regrettable and unfortunate that the state of New York has successfully prevented the Seminary from becoming an accredited institution of higher learning. We find it also regrettable that the intellectually open environment of the Seminary stands in sharp contrast to many of the other Unification Church centers of activity.

Rational Inquiry and Emotional Desperation

Rational or objective inquiry includes the practice of opening a view to critical analysis and evaluation. In addition, it includes the practice of opening wide the search for truth so that the inquirer may become exposed to other views and claims. Finally, the objective study of religion—or any subject—includes the practice of comparing rival views with one another rather than entertaining one view only. In short, objective investigation is the steady endeavor to *understand more than one view and to critically test each view.*

A religion uses unfair tactics to the extent that it uses guilt or social pressure to discourage a candidate from raising critical questions about the religion's claims.[16] Even if a convert has joined the religion of his own free choice (that is, because he desired to do so), the tactics of the religious group still stand morally condemned if the group fails to provide an open and critical learning environment. Such an environment would be a social setting in which the candidate or convert is encouraged to ask his own questions and to explore a variety of possible answers in addition to those offered by the group.

But, we hasten to add, people cannot live by rational inquiry alone. They have emotional needs, some of which may be so strong and unfulfilled as to cripple their ability to inquire critically and objectively into any religious view. A drowning individual is not likely to let a loose plank float past him just because he has not examined it thoroughly and carefully. Indeed, he would be irrational not to reach for it if he can see no better object to lock onto. When people act out of desperation, they may look upon careful, objective inquiry as a luxury they cannot afford.

In turn, a convert may begin to see at least vaguely that a decision once made in extreme desperation cannot be carried out indefinitely without some major revisions. That is why ordinarily converts eventually begin to think more objectively about their religion if they feel that they are no longer in a condition of desperation. Unfortunately, some religious groups

---

[16]See William Warren Bartley III, *The Retreat to Commitment, pp. 219-20.*

make it quite difficult for their members to entertain doubts, new options, or unapproved questions.

We join those who are severely critical of religious groups that seem virtually to seduce desperate people into their fold. We deplore the groups' unfair tactics and their disrespect for human dignity and intelligence. However, lest our righteous indignation be transformed into self-righteousness, we must move quickly to add that to fail to be sensitive to people who are in a state of religious desperation is also to show disrespect for their human dignity. There is no reason why religious groups cannot be zealous both to offer support and aid to those suffering finitude-shock and to provide them a secure environment in which objective and rational inquiry about religion can develop without discouragement or excessive delay.

It is difficult to cultivate both a concern for the individual's intellectual integrity and a concern for the emotional dimension of his religious needs. But if those two concerns continue to be isolated from each other as much as they have in the recent past, we may expect the future to continue to supply us with religious conversions either steeped in irrationality or void of profound feeling and celebration.

Bibliography

Below are listed some of the books and articles that we have consulted in our research. A few of the books list other important and appropriate bibliographical entries.

Ackermann, Robert John. *The Philosophy of Karl Popper.* Amherst: University of Massachusetts Press, 1976.

Albright, W. F. *From the Stone Age to Christianity.* 2nd ed. Garden City, N.Y.: Anchor Books, Doubleday, 1957.

Barber, Bernard. *Science and the Social Order.* Chicago: The Free Press of Glencoe, 1952.

Barnhart, J. E. "Reductionism and Religious Explanation." *Perspectives in Religious Studies,* 4:3 (Fall 1977).

———, *Religion and the Challenge of Philosophy.* Totowa, New Jersey: Littlefield, Adams and Co., 1975.

———, *The Billy Graham Religion.* Philadelphia: Pilgrim Press, 1972.

———, *The Study of Religion and Its Meaning.* New York: Walter de Gruyter, Inc., 1977.

Barnhart, Mary Ann. "Religion and Society: A Comparison of Selected Works of Emile Durkheim and Max Weber." Unpublished thesis, North Texas State University, 1967.

Bartley, William W., III. *The Retreat to Commitment.* New York: Alfred A. Knopf, 1962.

Beam, James Michael. "Billy Graham: 'I Can't Play God Anymore'." *McCall's Magazine* 105:4 (January 1978).

Beegle, Dewey M. *Scripture, Tradition, and Infallibility.* Grand Rapids: Eerdmans, 1973.

Bergson, Henri. *The Two Sources of Morality and Religion.* Translated by R. A. Audra and C. Brereton. Garden City, N.Y.: Doubleday Anchor Books, 1956.

Bromley, David G. and Anson D. Shupe, Jr. *"Moonies" in America: Cult, Church, and Crusade.* Beverly Hills: Sage Publications, 1979.

——— (see below, Shupe, Anson).

Brunner, Emil. *The Christian Doctrine of Creation and Redemption, Dogmatics,* vol. 2. Translated by Olive Wyon. London: Lutterworth Press, 1952.

Campbell, Joseph, ed. *Myths, Dreams, and Religion*. New York: E.P. Dutton, 1970.

Čapek, Milič. *Philosophical Impact of Contemporary Physics*. Princeton, N.J.: D. Van Nostrand Co., 1961.

Carnell, E. J. *The Case for Orthodox Theology*. Philadelphia: The Westminster Press, 1959.

Collins, Randall and Michael Makowsky. *The Discovery of Society*. New York: Random House, 1972.

Colson, Charles W. *Born Again*. New York: Bantam Press, 1976.

Cornelius, Benjamin. *Science, Technology, and Human Values*. Columbia: University of Missouri Press, 1965.

Crossman, Richard, ed. *The God that Failed*. New York: Bantam Books, 1952.

Davis, Stephen T. *The Debate About the Bible: Inerrancy Versus Infallibility*. Philadelphia: The Westminster Press, 1977.

Day, Richard E. *Bush Aglow: The Life Story of Dwight Lyman Moody*. Philadelphia: The Judson Press, 1936.

Dewey, John. *A Common Faith*. New Haven: Yale University Press, 1934.

"Dr. Graham: 'I Used to Play God'—New View Change," *The Texas Methodist* 124:30 (6 January 1978).

Durkheim, Emile. *The Elementary Forms of the Religious Life*. Translated by J. W. Swain. London: George Allen and Unwin Ltd., 1915.

Edwards, Cliff. *Biblical Christian Marriage*. Atlanta: John Knox Press, 1977.

Edwards, Jonathan. *Freedom of the Will*. Edited by Paul Ramsey. New Haven: Yale University Press, 1957.

_____ *Narrative of Many Surprising Conversions in Northampton and Vicinity: Together with Some Thoughts on the Revival of Religion in New England*. Worcester, Mass., 1832.

Eliade, Mircea. *Rites and Symbols of Initiation: The Mysteries of Birth and Rebirth*. Translated by W. R. Trask. New York: Harper and Row Torchbooks, 1958.

Enroth, Ronald. *Youth, Brainwashing, and the Extremist Cults*. Grand Rapids: Zondervan, 1977.

Evans, Richard I. *B. F. Skinner, The Man and His Ideas*. New York: E.P. Dutton and Company, 1968.

Feyerabend, Paul K. *Against Method*. London: Verso; New York: Schocken Books, 1975.

Frankl, Victor. *Man's Search for Meaning: An Introduction to Logotherapy*. Translated by Ilse Lasch. Boston: Beacon Press, 1962.

Fuller, B.A.G. *A History of Philosophy*. 2 vols. 3rd ed. Revised by Sterling M. McMurrin. New York: Holt, Rinehart and Winston, 1960.

Garre, Walter J. *The Psychotic Animal: A Psychiatrist's Study of Human Delusion*. New York: Human Sciences Press, 1976.

Gaustad, Edwin Scott. *Dissent in American Religion*. Chicago: University of Chicago Press, 1973.

Geertz, Clifford. *The Interpretation of Cultures*. Selected Essays. New York: Basic Books, 1973.

Gellner, Ernest. "Concepts and Society," *Rationality: Key Concepts in the Social Sciences*. Edited by Bryan R. Wilson. New York: Harper and Row, 1970.

Graham, Billy. *How to Be Born Again*. Waco, Texas: Word Books, 1977.

———. *Peace with God*. New York: Pocket Books, 1965.

Greeley, Andrew M. *The Jesus Myth: New Insights into the Person and Message of Jesus*. Garden City, N.Y.: Image Books, Doubleday, 1973.

Hanayama, Shoya. "Buddhism." In *The Meaning of Life in Five Great Religions*. Edited by R.C. Chalmen and John A. Irving. Philadelphia: The Westminster Press, 1965.

Hartshorne, Charles. *The Divine Relativity: A Social Conception of God*. New Haven: Yale University Press, 1948.

Hoebel, E. Adamson. *Anthropology: The Study of Man*. 3rd ed. New York: McGraw-Hill Book Co., 1958.

Horton, Robin. "African Traditional Thought and Western Science." *Africa*, 37 (1969).

Hunt, Morton. *The Affair: A Portrait of Extra-Marital Love in Contemporary America*. New York: World Publishing Co., 1969.

James, William. *The Varieties of Religious Experience: A Study in Human Nature*. New York: Modern Library, 1902.

Jaynes, Julian. *The Origin of Consciousness in the Breakdown of the Bicameral Mind*. Boston: Houghton Mifflin Co., 1977.

Jayson, L.N. *Mania*. New York: Funk and Wagnall, 1937.

Jeremias, Joachim. *New Testament Theology. Part I. The Proclamation of Jesus*. Translated by J. Bowden. London: SCM, 1971.

Jones, James W. "Reflections on the Problem of Religious Experience." *Journal of the American Academy of Religion* 40:4 (December 1972).

Kee, Howard Clark. *Christian Origins in Sociological Perspective: Methods and Resources*. Philadelphia: The Westminster Press, 1980.

―――― *Community of the New Age: Studies in Mark's Gospel*. Philadelphia: The Westminster Press, 1977.

Koch, Kurt. *Victory Through Persecution*. Grand Rapids: Kregel Publications, 1972.

Kuhn, Thomas. *The Structure of Scientific Revolutions*. 2nd ed. Chicago: University of Chicago Press, 1970.

Küng, Hans. *Infallible? An Inquiry*. Translated by Edward Quinn. Garden City, N.Y.: Doubleday, 1971.

La Barre, Weston. *The Ghost Dance: Origins of Religion*. New York: Dell Publishing Co., 1970.

Lakatos, Imre and Alan Musgrave, eds. *Criticism and the Growth of Knowledge: Proceedings of the International Colloquium in the Philosophy of Science, London, 1965*. Vol. 4. New York: Cambridge University Press, 1970.

MacIntyre, Alasdair. *Against the Self-Images of the Age: Essays on Ideology and Philosophy*. New York: Schocken Books, 1971.

McGuire, Meredith B. "Testimony as a Commitment Mechanism in Catholic Pentecostal Prayer Groups." *Journal for the Scientific Study of Religion* 16:2 (June 1977).

McNamara, Patrick H., ed. *Religion American Style*. New York: Harper and Row, 1974.

Moyer, Kenneth E. "Kinds of Aggression and their Physiological Basis." *Communications in Behavioral Biology*. Abstract No. 08680058, part A, 2 (1968). Cited in Perry London, *Behavior Control*. New York: Harper and Row, 1969.

Newman, John Henry. *Apologia Pro Vita Sua*. Garden City, N.Y.: Image Books, Doubleday, 1956.

Newman, William M., ed. *The Social Meanings of Religion*. Chicago: Rand McNally, 1974.

Nielsen, Kai. "Religiosity and Powerlessness." *The Humanist* 37:3 (May/June 1977).

Oates, Wayne E. *The Psychology of Religion*. Waco, Texas: Word Books, 1973.

Pache, René. *The Inspiration and Authority of Scripture.* Translated by Helen I. Needham. Chicago: Moody Press, 1969.

Perry, John W. *Roots of Renewal in Myth and Madness: The Meaning of Psychotic Episodes.* San Francisco: Jossey-Bass Publishers, 1976.

Pierard, R.V. "Billy Graham and the U.S. Presidency." *Journal of Church and State* 22:1 (Winter 1980).

Pinnock, Clark. *Biblical Revelation: The Foundation of Christian Theology.* Chicago: Moody Press, 1971.

Pruyser, Paul W. "Problems of Definition and Conception in the Psychological Study of Unbelief." In *Changing Perspectives in the Scientific Study of Religion.* Edited by Allan W. Eister. New York: John Wiley and Sons, 1974.

Ramm, Bernard. *Patterns of Religious Authority.* Grand Rapids: Eerdmans, 1961.

Reese, William L. and Eugene Freeman, eds. *Process and Divinity: The Hartshorne Festschrift.* Lasalle, Ill.: Open Court, 1964.

Renan, Ernest. *Recollections of My Youth.* Translated by C.B. Pitman. London: George Routledge & Sons, 1929.

Rhinehard, Luke. *The Book of est.* New York: Holt, Rinehart and Winston, 1976.

Ruo-Wang, Bao (Jean Pasqualine) and Rudolph Clelminski. *Prisoner of Mao.* New York: Coward McCann and Geoghegan, Inc., 1973.

Sanders, Jack T. *Ethics in the New Testament: Change and Development.* Philadelphia: Fortress Press, 1975.

Schnaitler, Roger. "Private Causes." *Behaviorism: A Forum for Critical Discussion* 6:1 (Spring 1979).

Sebald, Hans. *Witchcraft: The Heritage of a Heresy.* New York: Elsevier, 1978.

Settle, Tom. "Is Scientific Knowledge Rationally Justified?" in *Basic Issues in the Philosophy of Science.* Edited by W.R. Shea. New York: Science History Publications, 1976.

Settle, Tom, I.C. Jarvie and Joseph Agassi. "Towards a Theory of Openness to Criticism." *Philosophy of Social Science* 4 (1974).

Shupe, Anson D., Jr. and David G. Bromley. *The New Vigilantes: Deprogrammers, Anti-Cultists, and the New Religions.* Beverly Hills: Sage Publications, 1980.

———— (See above, Bromley, David).

Skinner, B.F. *About Behaviorism.* New York: Alfred A. Knopf, 1974.

Solomon, Philip, and others, eds. *Sensory Deprivation: A Symposium Held at Harvard Medical School.* Cambridge, Mass.: Harvard University Press, 1961.

Sontag, Frederick. *Sun Myung Moon and the Unification Church*. Nashville: Abingdon, 1977.

Taylor, John F.A. *The Masks of Society: An Inquiry into the Covenants of Civilization*. New York: Appleton-Century-Crofts, 1966.

Thomson, G.T. and F. Davidson. "The Epistle to the Romans." In *The New Bible Commentary*. 2nd ed. Edited by F. Davidson. Grand Rapids: Eerdmans, 1954.

Trigg, Roger. *Reason and Commitment*. New York: Cambridge University Press, 1973.

Truzzi, Marcello, ed. *VERSTEHEN: Subjective Understanding in the Social Sciences*. Reading, Mass.: Addison-Wesley Publishing Co., 1974.

Tsanoff, Radoslav A. *Autobiographies of Ten Religious Leaders: Alternatives in Christian Experience*. San Antonio: Trinity University Press, 1968.

van Baaren, Th.P. and H.J.W. Drijvers, eds. *Religion, Culture and Methodology: Papers of the Groningen Working-group for the Study of Fundamental Problems and Methods of Science of Religion*. The Hague/Paris: Mouton, 1973.

van Gennep, Arnold. *The Rites of Passage*. Translated by M.A. Vizedom and G.L. Caffee. Chicago: University of Chicago Press, 1960.

Ward, Wilfred. *The Life of John Henry Cardinal Newman*. Vol. 2. London: Longmans, Green, 1927.

Wash, Renee. "Entertainer George Hamilton IV." *Baptist and Reflector* 46:15 (16 April 1980).

Weber, Max. *The Sociology of Religion*. Translated by Talcott Parsons. Boston: Beacon Press, 1922.

Wells, G.A. *The Jesus of the Early Christians: A Study in Christian Origins*. Buffalo, N.Y.: Prometheus Books, 1971.

Wesley, John. *The Journal of the Rev. John Wesley, A.M.* Edited by Nehemiah Curnock. London: The Epworth Press, 1938.

White, L.A. *The Science of Culture: A Study of Man and Civilization*. New York: Farrar, Straus and Giroux, 1949.

Whitehead, A.N. *Religion in the Making*. New York: Living Age, Meridian Books, Inc., 1960.

Whiteley, C.H. "Mental Causes." In *The Human Agent. Royal Institute of Philosophy Lectures*. Vol. 1, 1966-67. New York: St. Martin's Press, 1968.

Wilson, Edward O. *Sociobiology: The New Synthesis*. Cambridge, Mass: Belknap Press of Harvard University Press, 1975.

Yinger, J. Milton. *The Scientific Study of Religion.* New York: Macmillan Co., 1970.

Zaehner, R.C. "Why Not Islam?" *Religious Studies* 11:2 (June 1975).

Author Index

Albright, William F., 111
Ambrose, 77
Amos, 59
Augustine, 77

Babcock, Maltbie D., 134
Barber, Bernard, 56
Barnhart, Joe E., 17, 108, 155, 162
Barnhart, Mary Ann, 75
Bartley, William W. III, 153, 163
Beam, James Michael, 15
Beegle, Dewey M., 30, 54
Bergson, Henri, 73, 96
Bright, Bill, 16
Bromley, David, 10, 125, 146, 148
Brunner, Emil, 54

Campbell, Joseph, 127
Capet, Milic, 45
Carnell, E. J., 86, 87
Collins, Randall, 79
Colson, Charles W., 25, 26, 99, 106, 133
Cornelius, Benjamin, 56
Crossman, Richard, 11

Darwin, Charles, 79
Davidson, F., 43
Davis, Stephen T., 88
Day, Richard E., 132
Dewey, John, 78, 80
Dodd, Charles H., 43
Durkheim, Emile, 71, 74, 78, 79, 94, 95, 96
Durst, Martin Irwin ("Mose"), 146, 146

Eddy, Mary Baker, 46
Edwards, Cliff, 78
Edwards, Jonathan, 59, 133, 157
Einstein, Albert, 107, 118
Eliade, Mircea, 2, 23
Enroth, Ronald, 11
Evans, Richard I., 157

Feyerabend, Paul K., 153
Finney, R. E. Jr., 5
Frankl, Victor, 138
Freud, Sigmund, 74
Fuller, B. A. G., 126

Gamaliel, 30
Garre, Walter J., 74
Gellner, Ernest, 85
Graham, Billy, 14, 15, 16, 17, 18, 105, 106, 129, 130
Greeley, Andrew M., 42

Hanayama, Shoyu, 28
Hartshorne, Charles, 105
Heraclitus, 2
Heisenberg, Werner, 44
Hoebel, E. Adamson, 26
Horton, Robin, 153
Hughes, Harold, 27
Hunt, Morton, 128, 130, 134, 139

Isaiah, 28

James, William, 49
Jaynes, Julian, 57, 58, 61, 68, 69, 88, 89, 92
Jayson, L. N., 59
Jeremiah, 59, 60
Jeremias, Joachim, 61
John, The Apostle, 77
John XXIII, Pope, 42
Jones, James W., 134

Kahal, Irving, 133
Kee, Howard Clark, 65
Kekule, F. A., 56
Koch, Kurt, 14
Koestler, Arthur, 29
Kuhn, Thomas, 44, 107

Lakatos, Imre, 108
Lerner, Alan Jay, 131

Little, Winston W., 146
London, Perry, 156
Luther, Martin, 35

McGuire, Meredith, 137
MacIntyre, Alasdair, 142
Makowsky, Michael, 79
Mancuso, James C., 57
Marx, Karl, 11
Matthew, Saint, 80
Mead, George Herbert, 79
Mill, John Stuart, 150
Miller, William, 138
Moody, D. L., 132
Moon, Sun Myung, 10, 12, 13, 14, 68, 69,
    70, 98, 147, 148, 151, 162
Moses, 59
Moyer, Kenneth E., 156
Muhammad, 12
Musgrave, Alan, 108

Newman, John Henry, 32, 33, 34, 35, 36,
    37, 38, 40, 41, 48, 57, 140
Nielsen, Kai, 81

Oates, Wayne E., 154

Pache, René, 84, 85
Paul, the Apostle, 6, 16, 42, 43, 44, 53, 57,
    62, 63, 64, 65, 66, 67, 68, 69, 97, 101,
    107, 108, 109, 110, 112, 113, 114,
    115, 116, 118, 119, 160
Pauli, Wolfgang, 44, 56
Perry, Johm W., 115
Peter, The Apostle, 52, 53, 60, 66, 67, 87,
    114
Pierard, Richard V., 17
Pinnock, Charles, 31
Plantinga, Alvin, 105,
Plato, 2
Pruyser, Paul W., 47

Ramm, Bernard, 85, 86
Renan, Ernest, 32, 33, 38, 39, 40, 41, 42,
    48, 57

Rhinehart, Luke, 37
Richardson, Herbert, 12, 68
Ruo-Wang, Bao, 154
Russell, Charles Taze, 139

Sanders, Jack T., 87
Sarbin, Theodore R., 57
Savad, Mark, 132
Schleiermacher, 24, 96
Schnaitler, Roger, 48
Schweitzer, Albert, 41
Settle, Tom, 153
Shupe, Anson, Jr., 10, 125, 146, 148
Skinner, B. F., 157, 158
Solomon, Philip, 152
Sontag, Frederick, 12
Stein, Joseph, 62
Stendahl, Krister, 42
Szasz, Thomas, S., 57

Tennor, Dorothy, 136
Thomson, G. T., 43
Trigg, Roger, 153
Tsanoff, Radoslav, 39, 40

Van Gennep, Arnold, 90, 91
Voltaire, 136

Ward, Wilfred, 36, 37
Wash, Renee, 148
Weber, Max, 3, 63, 79, 93, 94, 117
Wells, G. A., 116
Wesley, John, 32, 35, 36, 37, 48, 57
White, L. A., 94
Whitehead, A. N., 84, 85
Whiteley, C. H., 159
Williams, Roger, 81
Willson, Meredith, 132
Wilson, Edward, 99

Yinger, J. Milton, 22

Zaehner, R. C., 30